UNDERGROUND CLASSICS

The TRANSFORMATION of COMICS into COMIX

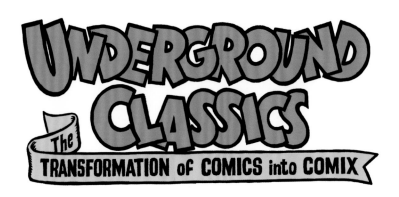

LAST GASP
BINKY BROWN
50¢
YOUNGSTERS PROHIBITED
meets The Holy
Virgin Mary
SPEAK, MY SON.
BUT- MY THOUGHTS
NO!
IMPURE THOUGHTS
NO!
B
JUSTIN GREEN

No longer burdened by pretentious notions of making "art," I am concerned with refining and communicating specific ideas of changing others' consciousness. This is pretentious, but it's much more fun.

—JUSTIN GREEN

SLOW DEATH

LAST GASP

Nº 2

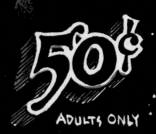

50¢

ADULTS ONLY

Comics are only one aspect of art for me. You pick the medium that will best express what you have to say, right? It just happens that comics are one of the best mediums.

—JACK JACKSON

CORN
NO. 2
CARTOONISTS CO-OP PRESS
LOCAL NO. 1
U C W OF A
FED
COMICS
ADULTS ONLY!
IN THIS ISSUE! MAJOR SECRETS OF THE UNIVERSE EXPOSED IN ... "MILES MICROFT'S LAST CASE!"
MORE ENTERTAINMENT THAN YOU THOUGHT YOU COULD STILL GET FOR ...
50¢
Kim Deitch

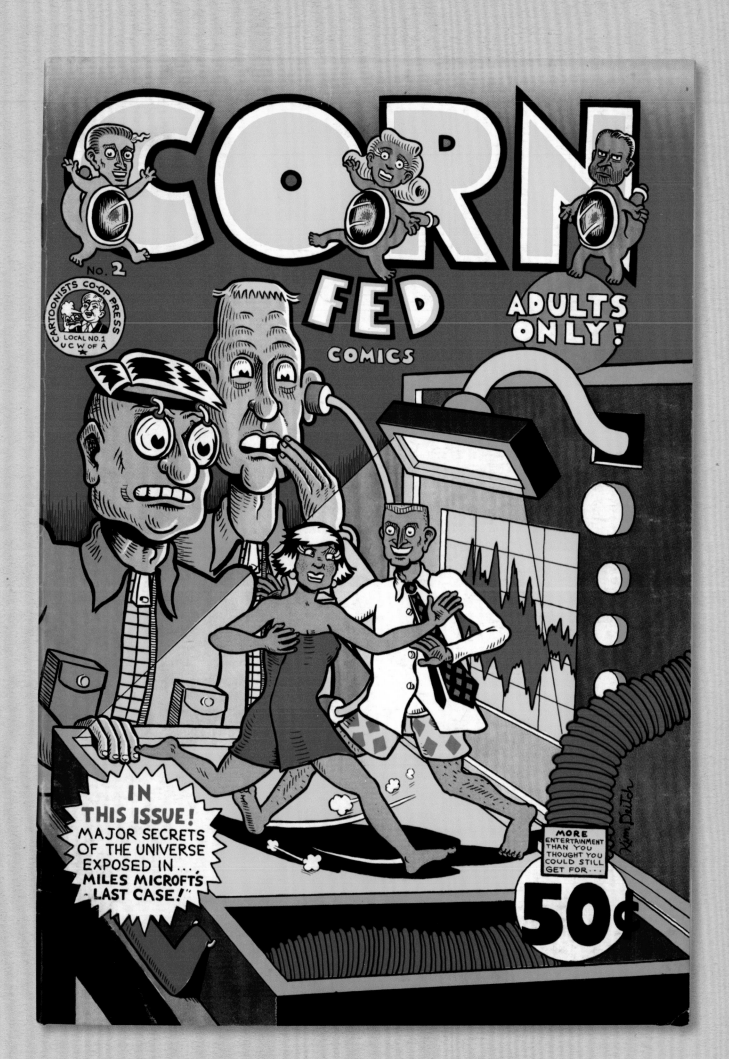

What I'm basically trying to do is tell good stories, and when I'm working, I give virtually everything I've got to that cause.

—KIM DEITCH

ZAP
COMIX
American
Flyer FUNNIES
young
young
BIJOU
Tales of
TOAD
50¢

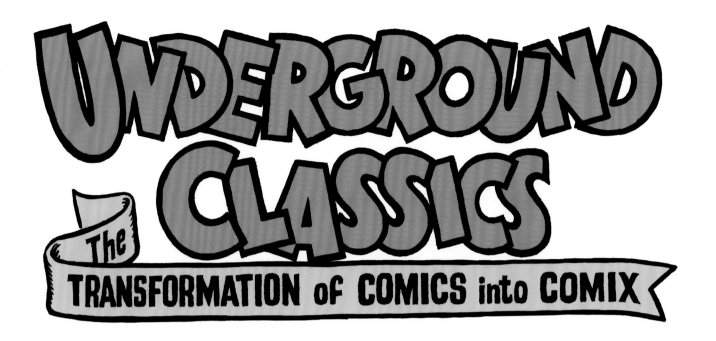

By James Danky and Denis Kitchen

Introduction by Jay Lynch

Designed by Kitchen, Lind & Associates

Abrams ComicArts
New York
in association with the
Chazen Museum of Art

Project Manager: Charles Kochman
Editor: Eric Klopfer
Designers: Greg Sadowski, John Lind for Kitchen, Lind & Associates
Art Director: John Lind
Production Manager: Alison Gervais

Library of Congress Cataloging-in-Publication Data

Danky, James Philip, 1947–
  Underground classics : the transformation of comics into comix, 1963–1990 /
by James P. Danky and Denis Kitchen.
    p. cm.
  ISBN 978-0-8109-0598-6 (Harry N. Abrams, Inc.)
  1. Underground comic books, strips, etc.—United States—History and
criticism. I. Kitchen, Denis, 1946- II. Chazen Museum of Art. III. Title.

NC1764.5.U6D36 2009
741.5'97309045—dc22
              2008030382

This book was produced for Harry N. Abrams, Inc., by Kitchen, Lind & Associates, LLC.
www.kitchenandlind.com

Published in 2009 by Abrams ComicArts, an imprint of Harry N. Abrams, Inc. All rights
reserved. No portion of this book may be reproduced, stored in a retrieval system, or
transmitted in any form or by any means, mechanical, electronic, photocopying, recording,
or otherwise, without written permission from the publisher.

Printed and bound in China
10 9 8 7 6 5 4 3 2 1

Abrams ComicArts books are available at special discounts when purchased in quantity
for premiums and promotions as well as fundraising or educational use. Special editions
can also be created to specification. For details, contact specialmarkets@hnabooks.com
or the address below.

HNA ▪▪▪▪▪
harry n. abrams, inc.
a subsidiary of La Martinière Groupe
115 West 18th Street
New York, NY 10011
www.hnabooks.com

For Christine, who has had to hear about this project for years and has
been supportive all along. Finally a book with pictures. — James Danky

To my old colleagues in the underground trenches, some of whom are no
longer with us, but most of whom are still raising hell. — Denis Kitchen

ACKNOWLEDGMENTS

The Underground Classics exhibit at the Chazen Museum of Art would have
remained a dream without the early enthusiasm of Russell Panczenko, director
of the Chazen Museum of Art. Chazen staffers Mary Ann Fitzgerald, Susan
Day, and Jerl Richmond were essential to the project and we thank them.

   When we planned the exhibit and book, we knew we had to talk to Eric
Sack. Eric has possibly the largest collection of original underground comix art,
and he is the most generous and cooperative of lenders, motivated by wanting
to share what he is passionate about. We also thank the individual collectors,
artists, and widows who loaned work, in particular among them Howard Cruse,
Gary Hallgren, Martha Holmes, Tina and Sam Jackson, and Jay Kinney.

   Thanks to all the folks at Harry N. Abrams, Inc., in particular
Executive Editor Charlie Kochman, whose new Abrams ComicArts imprint
is a perfect home for this book, Editor Eric Klopfer, for his dedication to
this project and willingness to assist at all crossroads, Publisher Steve Tager
for getting the ball rolling, Managing Editor Andrea Colvin, and Alison
Gervais in production.

   On the design side, we consider ourselves lucky to have had the always
dedicated John Lind serve as art director and co-designer for this book.
Kitchen, Lind & Associates was also fortunate in then being able to enlist
designer Greg Sadowski. In addition to their respective design talents,
each of them had helpful editorial advice and considerable expertise regarding
comix and the underground artists from the era, which proved invaluable.

   We realized the need for getting the voice of the comix artist into the
book to go along with the art. Jay Lynch's brilliant introduction and sense
of cultural history sets the stage for the art that follows.

   To help interpret the visual world of comix requires words, and in that
regard we have been exceptionally fortunate to have friends who are experts.

   Our first call was to Paul Buhle, who teaches in the American Civilization
Department at Brown University and has authored and edited dozens of books,
several on comics.

   Pat Rosenkranz has been terrifically helpful previewing the book
(though any errors are still ours!). Pat's *Rebel Visions* is the essential volume
that lays out the history of comix in four-color detail.

   It would not have been conceivable to think about comix without Trina
Robbins. Trina is not only a critical artist for the exhibit and this volume but
also the author of crucial texts that make the historical record of women in
comics accessible.

   Peter Poplaski, another artist in this book and exhibit, created the
distinctive logo and other lettering for the book cover, in conjunction with
Robert Crumb, who generously permitted use of his art for the cover.

   We are also grateful to the following individuals: E. B. Boatner and
Pat Rosenkranz for some of the artist photographs appearing in the book;
David Miller and Carol Kossack (representing the estate of Clay Geerdes);
Kevin Downey for photographing much of the original art; Mark Estren, for
being there first with *A History of Underground Comix*; Stacey Kitchen for the
production assistance; Dave Dumas at Pivot Media; Paul Hass, for early support
and edits; and Leonard Rifas for his perspective, understanding, and friendship.

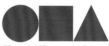

Chazen Museum of Art

Underground Classics: The Transformation of Comics
into Comix exhibiton originated with the Chazen Museum
of Art in Madison, Wisconsin, in spring 2009.

Front endpaper | Peter Poplaski, detail from *Comix Book* no. 1, cover, 1973
Page 2 | Justin Green, *Binky Brown Meets the Holy Virgin Mary*, cover, 1972
Page 4 | Jack Jackson, *Slow Death* no. 2, cover, 1970
Page 6 | Kim Deitch, *Corn Fed Comics* no. 2, cover, 1973
Page 8 | Patrick Rosenkranz, photograph of comix at Print Mint, 1972
Page 11 | Robert Crumb, detail from *Home Grown Funnies* no. 2, cover, 1972
Page 144 | Greg Irons, detail from *Slow Death Funnies* no. 1, cover, 1970
Back endpaper | Rand Holmes, detail from *A History of Underground Comics*, cover, 1973

CONTENTS

#3
KITCHEN SINK
50¢
BIJOU
funnies
ADULTS ONLY!
SAKES ALIVE! WHAT IS THAT PUDGY FELLOW DOING?
SAMMY SMOOT
NARD
HOLY KAZOOSIS! SOMEBODY STOP HIM! HE'S EATIN' TH' COVER!
BOB KLEEN
PAT
CONNIE LINGUS
CHOMP CHOMP CHOMP
RRRING!
1
LYNCH

Introduction
By Jay Lynch

IN 1959 I SAW MY FIRST COPY of Paul Krassner's magazine the *Realist*, and it completely blew me away. The *Realist* seemed to be publishing material that mirrored my own private thoughts on taboo topics as it zoomed in on the sham and hypocrisy of society at large. This was during the Eisenhower era, when such things just didn't see print. Yet here was a fellow at last publishing the TRUTH in his little magazine of "Freethought, Criticism, and Satire." Krassner's mentor was Lyle Stuart, and through the pages of the *Realist* I soon learned about Stuart's newspaper the *Independent*, another no-holds-barred paper that dared to speak the unspeakable. So by 1960 I was a subscriber to both these early forerunners of the underground press.

The *Realist* was it for me. When I first saw the magazine, it put me in a daze. I hadn't been so wigged-out over a publication since 1952, when I first saw Harvey Kurtzman's *MAD* comics. Through satire, *MAD* pointed out the foibles of our culture as well. But it was a comic book, after all. So it didn't get too deeply into the more gritty aspects of the societal problems of its day. But *MAD* was ahead of its time in '52. The title of the comic book itself—*MAD*—not only meant "insane." It also meant "angry!"

In an early *Realist*, Krassner printed a parody of L. Ron Hubbard's *Dianetics*. The piece was called *Epizootics*, and it was by Gershon Legman. It was reprinted from *Neurotica* magazine. *Neurotica* was published by Jay Landesman between 1948 and 1951. It was a little magazine with a small circulation. Yet in its day, it was the Bible of the Nervous Generation that *Time* magazine would later label the "beatniks," a term coined by *San Francisco Chronicle* columnist Herb Caen in 1958. The satellite *Sputnik* was in the news, so Caen simply added that Russian suffix to the first word of "Beat Generation." *Time* began using Caen's term "beatnick" in its articles, and the word was quickly absorbed into to the pop slang of late 1950s *Time*-speak. Legman's writings appeared frequently in *Neurotica*. And almost a decade before

Jack Kerouac's *On the Road* was published, *Neurotica* had its place on the orange-crate coffee tables of the disaffected young urban bohemians of the Beat Generation. Later, in 1954, Jay Landesman opened the Crystal Palace nightclub in St. Louis. And in 1959 he was one of the few risk-taking nightclub owners to book Lenny Bruce.

But back to *Time*'s penchant to add to the pop lexicon: It was *Time* that invented the label "underground newspapers" in a 1966 article about the phenomenon. Andy Warhol was known for his underground movies, and this inspired *Time*'s phrase. (Well—it could have been worse. At least they didn't call these groundbreaking publications "Warholniks.")

In 1965 LSD was legal and Timothy Leary was still wearing a suit (he hadn't donned the Nehru jacket and love beads yet). I was doing cartoons for the *Realist*, the *Idiot*, *Nexus*, and a bunch of other free-thought mags of the era. I tried LSD, and it was something all right. Charles Willoughby Smith, a beat poet chum, showed up at my doorstep one day in January 1966. His former bearded, sweatshirted beatnik look was gone. He was all clean-shaven now. "What's the deal?" I inquired. "I just decided I'd rather look like a sunrise than the Wolfman," Smith replied.

The old Beats slowly made the transition to hippiedom. And in '67, Gershon Legman wrote a book called *The Fake Revolt*, wherein Legman (the man who popularized the phrase "Make Love Not War" in 1963) severely criticized and chided the hippies for their lack of intellectualism and their penchant for submitting to hippie leaders rather than making their own decisions. So I guess I was forewarned.

I remember having many a Legman discussion in the early 1970s with Robert Crumb's then brother-in-law and fellow Chicagoan Marty Pahls. And given Marty and Robert's long list of mutual interests, I would postulate that Crumb was hip to Legman's critique of hippiedom early on as well.

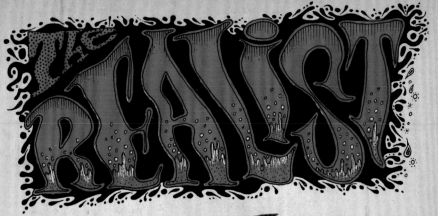

LEFT | JAY LYNCH
The Realist no. 76, cover, summer 1967.
PAUL KRASSNER's iconoclastic magazine was
an influence on many underground cartoonists.
For this issue, Lynch designed a psychedelic
version of its logo and "St. Realist" mascot.

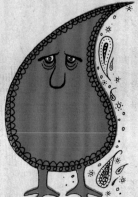

Case History of the Manchester Caper

by Paul Krassner

Once there was upon a time a face painted on the hand of Señor Wences that magically became a real person named Jacqueline. She kissed a senator in a Spearmint ad, and he in turn became a real person named Jack. They were married by Chief Justice Earl Warren and lived in good taste for not quite ever after.

Suddenly he was slain by the man who had most to gain — Mark Lane — who in turn was killed at the police station by Vaughn Meader.

(Continued on Page 13)

Legal and Actual Concentration Camps in America

by Charles R. Allen, Jr.

While fascism is many things, reflected in unnumbered manifestations, it is, quintessentially, the art of the end square—carried to a terrible science. Hitler, Mussolini, Trujillo, Batista, Franco—and, of course, today's variant, Johnson—were, and are, above all proto-type squares.

It's not only that each in his own way — Mussolini with his castor oil 'treatment,' Hitler with his concentration camp system leading directly to the 'Final Solution' (the last, desperate

(Continued on Page 5)

Blow-Up, Psychedelic Sexualis and The War Game —or, David Hemmings Is Herman Kahn in Disguise

Ready for another little trippypoo?

Start with this letter from a subscriber: "I've recently heard rumors that Paul Krassner doesn't exist and that he is, in fact, a composite of a number of fulsome individuals. These people, it's said, each subject themselves monthly to a strange experience, then everyone's experience is compiled into one story which is subsequently given some idiotic moral (much in the same way *Time* magazine writes its articles). In issue #74, for example, the *Crazy SANE to Loving Haight* story was actually written by a Krassner who attended SANE's rally, another who's an ascetic but takes acid, another who visited Haight-Ashbury, another who

reads *McCall's* ads in the N.Y. *Times*, another who insulted Joe Pyne, etc. In this way, the story appears to be the exploits of one man, the mythical Paul Krassner. I've also heard that a conspiracy has developed by which one faction of Paul Krassners is seeking to gain control over the rest through the use of CIA terror tactics. Is this the reason I haven't received issue #75?"

Now the whole world knows.

This has been Vietnam Summer, a men's cologne, more fragrant than Spring Mobilization, which sponsored an anti-war march on April 15, in San Francisco, where then-*Ramparts*-publisher-not-to-be Ed Keating

(Continued on Page 17)

No. 75

35 Cents

1965 and 1966 saw the flowering of Mario Savio's Free Speech Movement at the University of California, Berkeley. Joel Beck, a cartoonist for the Berkeley college humor magazine *Pelican*, began publishing a series of comical booklets known as *The Alienated War Baby Report*. These included titles like *Marching Marvin* and *Lenny of Laredo*. A year or two before that, Jack Jackson, a cartoonist for the University of Texas at Austin humor mag *Ranger*, published a comic book called *God Nose*. And even before that, another *Ranger* cartoonist, Frank Stack (using the nom de plume Foolbert Sturgeon), published his comic, *The Adventures of Jesus*, in 1964. But the first really successful underground comic, the first really popular post-acid underground comic, was Robert Crumb's *Zap Comix* no. 1, which came out in 1967.

Many of the early underground comix artists were in touch with one another from previous stages of their cartooning careers. Some we knew from the fanzines that we published as kids in the late fifties and early sixties. Some we knew from the college humor mags we did in the earlier part of the sixties. And more than a few of the early underground cartoonists, including

yours truly, were published in Harvey Kurtzman's *Help!* magazine in the early sixties as well.

When the underground newspapers took off in '67 or so, many of us did cartoons for the early underground press. My work ran in the *East Village Other*, the *Chicago Seed*, the *Berkeley Barb*, the *Fifth Estate*…the list goes on. In '67, Skip Williamson and I started an underground humor mag called the *Chicago Mirror*. By the third issue of the *Mirror*, we were getting a little bit discouraged, though. It seemed that the hippies just didn't seem to grasp the concept of satire. This was driven home to me one day when I was selling copies of the *Mirror* on the streets of Chicago's sixties hippie neighborhood known as Old Town.

At this time, the press had been reporting that some hippies had been drying and curing banana skins to smoke for a legal high. In the *Mirror* we ran a piece satirically stating that smoking dog poop would provide an excellent psychedelic experience. We went on to say that the best variety of poop was something called "Lincoln Park Brown," and we gave tongue-in-cheek instructions for preparing the poop for smoking. We said that the new breed of dog-poop smokers were known as "shit heads." Get it? "Pot heads"? "Shit heads"? It's satire, right? But then when I was selling the mag on the street, this hippie came up to me and said, "Hey, man! Thanks for the tip on how to cure dog poop! We've been smoking it all week, and it's *groovy*!" I tried to explain to the kid that it was satire and that he shouldn't *really* be smoking dog poop, but he wouldn't listen. Apparently he was too blissed out of his mind on the nitrogen content of dog feces to grasp my explanation.

This contact with one of my typical readers—the inability of our readership to appreciate satire—disillusioned me somewhat. Shortly thereafter, Crumb sent me a copy of *Zap* no. 1. I showed it to Williamson, and we agreed: Instead of publishing the *Chicago Mirror*, we would do a comic book. A few months later Crumb came to town and "crashed at my pad," as we used to say in those days. Together with Skip Williamson, Jay Kinney, and Crumb, I put together the first issue of *Bijou Funnies*.

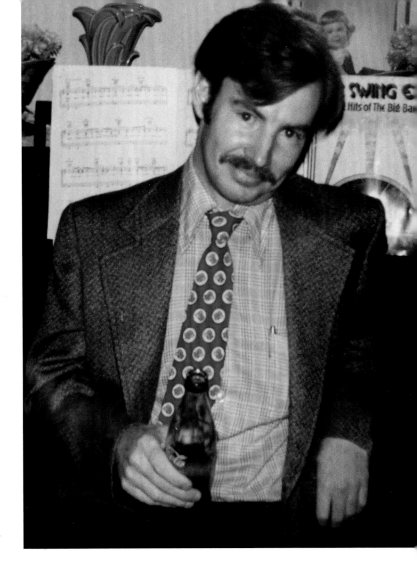

Gilbert Shelton was in Austin, Texas, then, doing cartoons for the underground paper there, the *Austin Rag*. I knew Shelton from *Help!* and from the college mags, and I wrote him soliciting a comics story for *Bijou* no. 1. Gilbert sent me some stuff and told me that he too was putting together an underground comic called *Feds 'N' Heads*. In the centerfold cartoon in *Feds 'N' Heads* no. 1, Shelton has one of his characters reading *Bijou*. But in fact, *Feds 'N' Heads* no. 1 and *Bijou* no. 1 were published at just about the same time, tying for the slot of the second post-acid underground comic ever published.

At first Crumb (in San Francisco), Shelton (in Austin), and me and Skip (in Chicago) distributed our own books. Eventually, though, Shelton moved to San Francisco. He and Robert made distribution deals with the Print Mint, a distributor of psychedelic rock posters and poetry mags, and Skip and I soon made a distribution deal with the Print Mint as well.

Shortly after *Bijou* no. 1 was published, I got a letter from Denis Kitchen in Milwaukee, Wisconsin, who was putting together *Mom's Homemade Comics* no. 1. A few months later, Crumb returned to Chicago, and we decided to take a bus up to Milwaukee (a mere eighty miles away) and check out this Kitchen dude.

Since Gilbert and Crumb were in San Francisco and lived just a hop, skip, and jump away from the Print Mint, they could go and collect their dough from those guys with ease. I was 2,000 miles away though. And *Bijou* was always the last to get paid. So somehow I talked Denis into distributing *Bijou*. And Crumb gave Denis *Home Grown Funnies* to publish. And pretty soon Denis was publishing a dozen titles. And other publishers sprang up. And there were more titles. By the early seventies there were hundreds of titles of these uncensored, black-and-white, so-called "underground comix."

Back then a regular Marvel or DC comic cost twelve cents. They were distributed on consignment, which meant that the newsdealer didn't have to shell out any dough up front. He would get the comics along with his bundle of other, more profitable mags, with fifty-cent cover prices on 'em. If the mag or comic sold, the newsdealer would pay a percentage of the retail price to the distributor. If the comic didn't sell, he would rip off the cover to prove the book didn't sell and return it to the distributor. Consignment distribution was originally instituted during the Great Depression as an incentive to newsdealers with a shortage of working capital. But it was the standard distribution method for the twelve-cent comic books in 1968.

Since your typical newsdealer has limited rack space, he would much sooner display a fifty-cent *Playboy* than a twelve-cent

Spider-Man. So the Marvel and DC books were basically "bundle padding"—the distributor would wrap the more lucrative mags in the cheap comics to protect them from getting bruised. And only a few dealers actually bothered to display the cheap bundle padding (i.e., comics) on their racks.

But the underground comix weren't typically newsstand items. They were sold in head shops and had a wholesale distribution system more akin to the way cigarette papers or bongs were being sold. They weren't consigned. They were wholesaled. This method of distribution later became known as "direct sales." And with the advent of original material being distributed to comic shops, it was this method of distribution, devised by the underground comix publishers, that eventually saved the entire comic book industry because in 1968, comic book shops were essentially used magazine stores. It wasn't until the mid-seventies that the "straight" publishers thought to print original material for direct sale to the comic shops.

Underground comix were the most important art movement of the twentieth century. Copies of many of the early books sell to collectors today for many thousands of dollars. It's all quite ironic. Rebellious cartoonists mocking consumer culture were inadvertently producing collectible artifacts for that same consumer culture forty years down the road. What can I say? All I can do is offer you readers some good advice: Whatever you do— *don't* try smoking dog poop! ∎

FAIR WARNING:
FOR ADULT INTELLECTUALS ONLY!
APPROVED BY THE GHOST WRITERS IN THE SKY
APEX NOVELTIES
all new
Zap
COMIX
NO.1
25¢
Zap Comics are Squinky Comics!!
I WISH SOMEBODY WOULD TELL ME WHAT "DIDDY-WAH-DIDDY" MEANS...
IF YOU DON'T KNOW BY NOW, LADY, DON'T MESS WITH IT!
WE GIVE ♡
SEE ROCK CITY
HEY, GET IT?
IS DIS A SYSTEM ?
Special Bonus!
KITCHEN KUT-OUTS!
MR. NATURAL VISITS THE CITY

Underground Classics
The Transformation of Comics into Comix, 1963–90
By James Danky and Denis Kitchen

DESPITE WHAT YOUR PARENTS MAY HAVE TOLD YOU, comics are not trash. Garish, sometimes tasteless or violent, frequently non-comical, yes—but they can also be needle-sharp, provocative, and brimming with fresh language and ideas. (Sorry, Mom.)

And contrary to what you've been told by pop-culture historians, comics did not exactly begin in the 1890s with the *Yellow Kid* or *Little Nemo*. As an art-driven storytelling medium, comics go back at least as far as the mid-nineteenth century and, arguably, to Goya, the Greek and Roman frescos, the Bayeaux Tapestry, and the cave walls of Lascaux.

Nor did comix, with that hip terminal "x," spring magically to life in 1968 with *Zap Comix* no.1 or *The Fabulous Furry Freak Brothers*. As with so many other art forms, "legitimate" or not, the evolution of comics is long, complex, and worthy of serious research and explication. (Sorry, man.)

As a subset of the comics genre, underground comix are indeed a product of the sixties. Like a new life-form, they were heaved up on shore during a decade of social and political turmoil, of changing societal and cultural norms. First came the "alternative" or "underground" newspapers. The editors of the *Los Angeles Free Press*, the *San Francisco Oracle*, the *East Village Other*, and thousands of similar papers nationwide combined a free-swinging journalistic style with a strong visual sense, attracting a small army of artists whose wild graphics and mind-boggling satire exploded in their pages as well as on concert posters, leaflets, T-shirts, and comic books. From San Francisco to Boston, from Milwaukee to Austin, the artists and editors of the undergrounds gleefully committed themselves to building the Movement, a new culture that embraced and endorsed the values of young Americans—namely, sex, drugs, and rock 'n' roll. (Did we mention there was a war on?)

While R. Crumb's *Zap* and Gilbert Shelton's *Freak Brothers* had the biggest national impact in terms of sales and popularity, artists like Frank Stack (aka Foolbert Sturgeon), Jack

OPPOSITE | ROBERT CRUMB
Zap Comix no. 1, cover, 1968
First printing by Charles Plymell

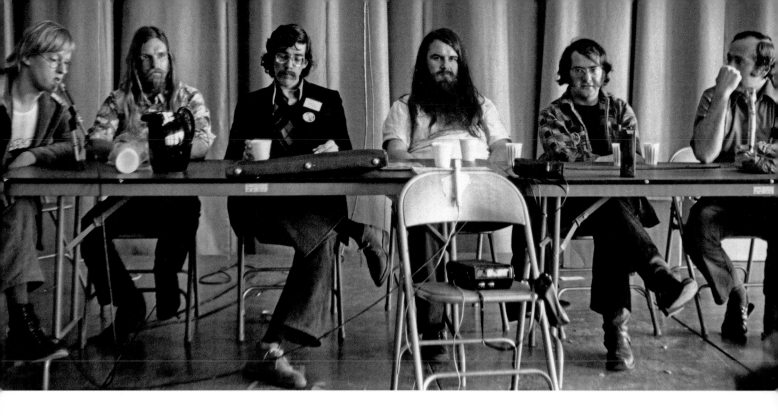

Jackson (Jaxon), and Joel Beck were the very first on the scene, producing underground comix of regional importance. Stack's nom de plume was a genuine ruse: He feared losing academic tenure (in the fine art department at the University of Missouri) if his association with comics became known. Jackson initially self-published the one-shot *God Nose* in 1964, before joining fellow Texan Shelton in founding Rip Off Press, Inc., in San Francisco. Beck initially responded to the free-speech movement in Berkeley.

As a new and bastard art form, underground comix found no natural or even pragmatic support outside the counterculture. Existing periodical distributors would have nothing to do with underground comix publishers, not only because much of the product was deemed pornographic, but also because of its anarchistic nature (and not just the content): There were no regular publishing schedules. So the Print Mint, Kitchen Sink Press (aka Krupp Comic Works), Last Gasp, and Rip Off Press (sometimes jokingly called, collectively, the "Big Four") carved a new distribution system based on head shops, flea markets, and hippie street-hawkers—retailers working the outermost fringes of American capitalism.

Underground comix were not treated as ordinary periodicals with a single month of life on a spinner rack. Comix were treated more as books with indefinite shelf lives. The bestselling underground titles were reprinted again and again, while weaker titles saw single printings. Mainstream comic book artists producing work-for-hire comics for companies like Marvel or DC were paid flat rates regardless of sales, but underground cartoonists maintained their copyrights and were paid royalties, like most literary authors. This meant that popular alternative cartoonists like Crumb and Shelton were relatively successful. But some compatriots, though well respected, maintained very marginal existences.

The demand for undergrounds swelled steadily in the early seventies. By 1973 *Freak Brothers* no. 1 alone had sold

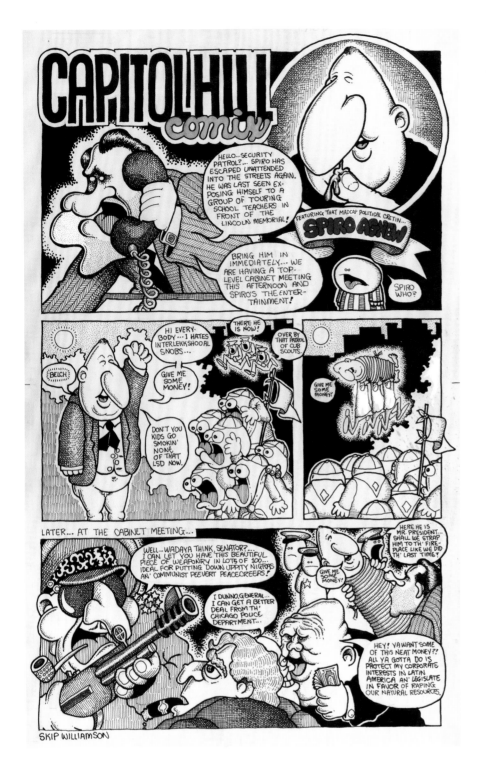

SKIP WILLIAMSON

retailers. That same year, the U.S. Supreme Court's "community standards" ruling in the *Miller v. California* case threw the definition of obscenity into local hands. The jurists' decision created a serious chill among the head-shop owners, who comprised the core distribution base for undergrounds. Already feeling politically vulnerable, these sellers of bongs, small wooden pipes, rolling papers, and other drug paraphernalia feared that comix would be the legal weak link allowing unfriendly city authorities to shut them down.

Faced with growing inventories and political paranoia, in 1973 large numbers of head shops and regional paraphernalia distributors dropped comix altogether. The surviving underground publishers and artists adapted through sheer stubbornness, diversification, and changing markets. Many saw the "crash of '73" as a necessary culling of the herd. And many of the genre's best and most lasting creations were yet to come.

When the divisive Vietnam War finally ended and the great party of the sixties and seventies broke up, the alternative press faced a major challenge. Many alternative newspapers folded; some firebrand editors became teachers or stockbrokers, and some comix artists went to work for ad agencies. But not all. Virtually anyone under thirty with the slightest consciousness of art and politics had by then heard of R. Crumb, Gilbert Shelton, Trina Robbins, Art Spiegelman, or other favorites—and had read some portion of the cacophony of comix being

400,000 copies, and the series, collectively, sold into the millions. Many of the most popular titles hit six-figure circulations. Publishers and hungry artists filled the vacuum, too often, with lesser, hastily assembled titles. Boom led inevitably to bust. In 1973 two independent factors dealt the cottage industry a double blow. The first was a direct result of the new distribution system. Traditional periodical distributors take returns on unsold magazines and comics, issue credits, and replace them with fresh titles. Books are traditionally sold to retailers on a returnable basis. Underground publishers ignored both entrenched systems. Their nontraditional wholesale accounts bought comix on a nonreturnable basis. Eventually the weakest titles created an inventory glut, even for the most discriminating

produced and passed along from reader to reader and from classes to dorm rooms to crash pads to communes.

There proved to be a continuing post-crash demand for the underground cartoonists' weird, unfettered, sex- and dope-crazed take on this American life. By then, too, both the artists and publishers had learned something about how to produce and market their diverse wares. The titles and niches proliferated: *Tales from the Leather Nun, Wet Satin: Women's Erotic Fantasies, Bizarre Sex,* and *Dope Comix* held lurid appeal, while titles like *Slow Death* or *Corporate Crime Comics* featured stories with political messages. *Gay Comix* and *Wimmen's Comix* often did both. Jack Jackson and Larry Gonick developed historical comics ranging in subject from Texas to the universe. Justin Green's idiosyncratic *Binky Brown Meets the Holy Virgin Mary* established what became another subgenre: autobiographical comics. Despite continuing blocked access to mainstream distributors, sales rebounded enough from the heights of the early 1970s to remain viable into the 1980s.

But in terms of self-expression, how can you distinguish the comix art produced on both coasts and in the Midwest during the 1960s? Artistically, the comix artists have roots in all manner of earlier paintings, drawings, and commercial work, including seminal comic books like Harvey Kurtzman's revolutionary *MAD* and *Humbug*. Aside from Kurtzman's humor titles, among the more immediate roots of the comix artists were E.C. Comics' horror and science-fiction titles, with their grotesque covers and fantastic, if frequently bloody, plots, all featuring the stellar cartoonists of their day.

Many of these very comics, important sources of inspiration for the vast majority of artists included in this exhibition, were condemned in the late 1950s by parental groups, congressional investigators, and the work of Dr. Fredric Wertham (*Seduction of the Innocent*), all of which cumulatively led to the creation of the industry's oppressive, self-censoring Comics Code Authority. As a result of this moral crusade, comic books in the 1950s, though loved by kids, came to be reviled by parents. And as these kids grew up, their parents almost invariably threw out those comics. During the late 1960s, the same grown readers were still interested in comics, but when they went looking for them, the E.C.s were extinct and the world of Archie and Veronica had changed dramatically. As an alternative to relatively anemic mainstream output, the undergrounds became a natural outlet for their curiosity.

Unfettered language, graphic depictions of sex, depictions and championing of recreational drug use, and the sometimes extreme violence in comix were alluring liberations for underground artists and readers alike, but it was also the literate choice of words, the unrestricted range of topics, and the wildly idiosyncratic drawing styles that truly distinguished and distanced comix from both their predecessors and their contemporary distant cousins on newsstands. Whether clean and simple, ugly and jarring, complex, psychedelic, or elegant, the styles of underground cartoonists are distinctive and recognizable: Each clearly shows an individual's distinct expression within the medium. Earlier cartoonists' influences can be seen in many cases, but the influences of larger art movements—Surrealism, Expressionism, Pointillism, forms of Abstractionism, and even Superrealism—are not without influence on this "art form that doesn't know its name."

Artists and writers who worked in the mainstream comic book industry of the day were typically older men who rarely

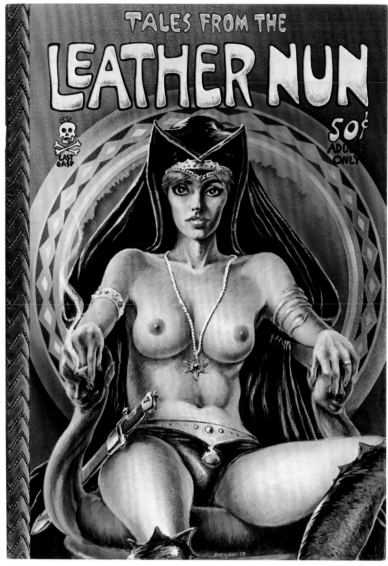

communicated with their younger audiences: Their output was largely contrived for a perceived market. Underground cartoonists were directly connected with their readership and shared generational values. There was a self-consciousness among the comix creators of what was being accomplished, an awareness unavoidable within a youth-driven counterculture largely focused on addressing the burning issues of the day: ending an unpopular war, legalizing marijuana, and supporting the rights of women, gays, and racial minorities. An "us vs. them" mentality was impossible to avoid in the polarized national climate of freaks and straights: Underground comix were decidedly not aimed at "them."

Comix—as was the case with earlier comic books—were mostly a guy thing; the essay by Trina Robbins in this volume is a reminder of their often one-sided gender dynamics. That said, prior to undergrounds, males overwhelmingly created and read comic books. Underground comix offered female artists the first true opportunity to enter the medium, and a far greater percentage of the underground cartoonists were female than had been in preceding generations. And for either gender, ids and topics had no bounds. With comix containing stories of relevance for women, more females than ever were attracted to

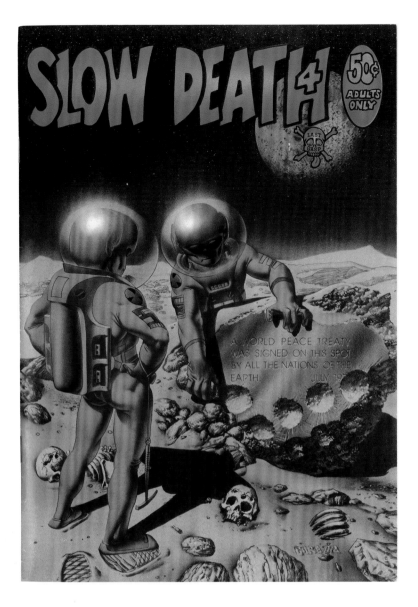

OPPOSITE | DAVE SHERIDAN
Tales from the Leather Nun, cover, 1973

LEFT | RICHARD CORBEN
Slow Death no. 4, cover, 1972

Today, some of these cheerfully demented comix and their offspring have made it into the mainstream or, at any rate, tributaries of the mainstream. They are no longer relegated to head shops or dimly lit comic stores; many are in public libraries, in Stuttgart as well as Sandusky. Collections of R. Crumb, Kim Deitch, and Art Spiegelman can be found on the shelves of Borders and Barnes & Noble—often right next to the Dungeons & Dragons stuff. (Bummer, man.) We hope that the struggle by comix artists and, by extension, their fans, to gain acceptance (not something that was a universal aspiration by any means) finds some resolution in this book.

WE ADD TWO FINAL NOTES, pertaining to the reproductions and to the selections, about the Underground Classics exhibition, which originated at the Chazen Museum of Art and which forms the foundation for this book.

The printed versions of comics and comix naturally stress clarity of line and legibility. In contrast, each drawing or painted illustration in this book has been photographed, without retouching, as an *object d'art*. Unlike their sanitized printed counterparts, the actual works are shown as intimate handmade objects, with smudges, masking tape, marginal notes, Wite-Out, registration crosshairs, and residual pencil lines as intrinsic, if ordinarily unseen, parts of the creative process.

Robert Crumb and Art Spiegelman have emerged as the preeminent artists of the underground comix movement. Their respective works have been widely published, honored, and exhibited in disproportion to their compatriots, so while they are certainly part of this exhibition and book, they do not dominate. A central purpose of the Underground Classics exhibition is to show the rich diversity of individuals and styles that comprise the movement, including many artists whose comix are largely out of print and seldom seen today. In addition, Harvey Kurtzman, Will Elder, and Will Eisner, three artists from an earlier generation, are included, not because they were direct participants in the underground comix movement, but because of their profound influence on many comix artists and because each produced the crossover works included here. The physical limitations of gallery space and catalogue pages make even this effort more limited in scope than is ideal, but it is expected that further exhibitions, both focused on underground comix subgenres and on single artists, will follow, as will further compilations and critical studies. ∎

the genre as readers. Similarly, comix welcomed gay cartoonists to come out of the closet, even if it was professionally dangerous for many to do so at the time.

The underground revolutions of the 1960s and 1970s, few more continuingly fascinating than comix, produced great social changes. From signal artists like Crumb, Spiegelman, Shelton, Bill Griffith, S. Clay Wilson, Spain Rodriguez, and so many more, the emerging culture found images and texts that communicated their thoughts and dreams and, sometimes, nightmares. The matrix of political, economic, technological, and artistic forces helped these artists, writers, and publishers connect to their readers, a connection that continues down to the present. Today, there are a vast group of young artists in America and internationally who grew up in the world that comix created. Their work takes for granted the freedoms established forty years ago.

The process of canonization, to which art museums greatly contribute, is an important aspect of advanced societies. Though not the only source of assigning value, this process is an important one. One can appreciate this process while being critical of the ways in which the state and its institutions approach culture. The process is also a lengthy one, where comix may be included once and excluded at a later date.

THE COLLECTED ADVENTURES OF
THE FABULOUS FURRY
FREAK BROTHERS
AMERICA
LOVE IT OR
50¢
TOOT TOOT
DOPE
Gilbert Shelton

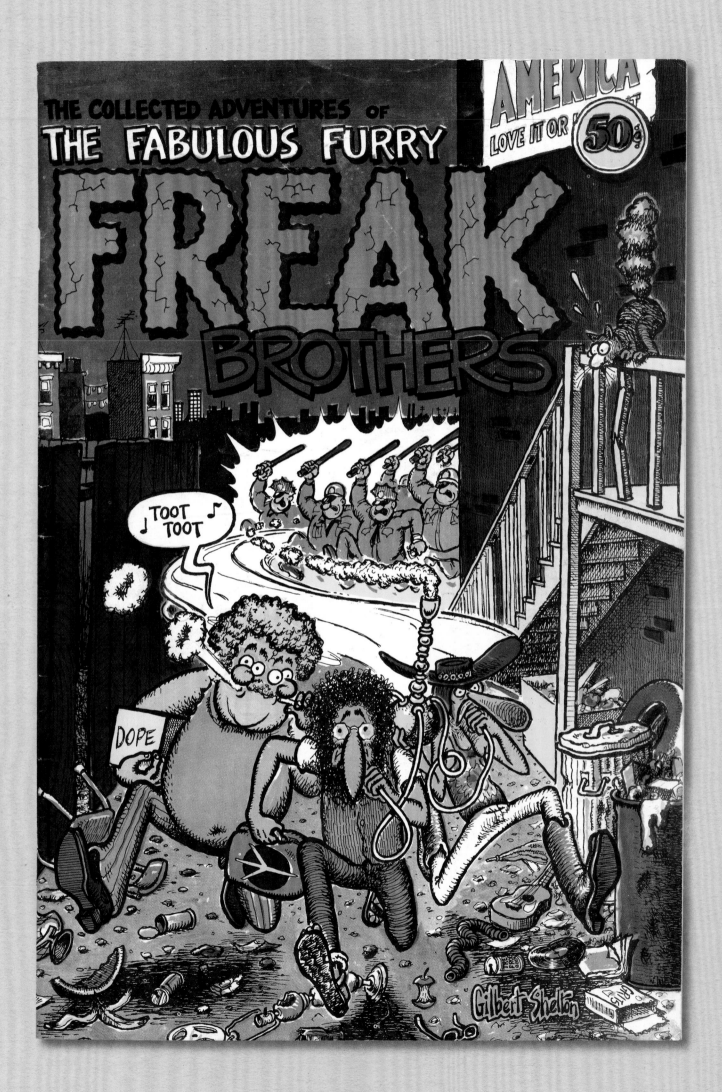

The Limited Legacy of Underground Comix
By Patrick Rosenkranz

Underground comix are more like art and less like comics.
—Gilbert Shelton

IT WAS A DETERMINED CADRE of cartoonists who precipitated one of the most revolutionary art movements of the twentieth century. Using the humble medium of comic books, the work they created—*Zap Comix, Young Lust, Mean Bitch Thrills, The Fabulous Furry Freak Brothers*, and many more—rearranged the comics landscape forever. For a brief time they became an ascendant force on the cultural zeitgeist, and a popular lifestyle accoutrement through the sheer audacity of the stories, the explicitness of the sex, and the wild-and-crazy graphic experimentation, along with a big "Fuck you if you don't like it!" to authority.

So why is it that, after all these years, underground comic books are undervalued, and not just in terms of how much they sell for on eBay? (It still doesn't make sense to me that a *Spider-Man* comic book from 1968 would sell for more than a *Feds 'N' Heads* from that same year, but that's not what I'm talking about.) It's almost like people want to forget them—a kind of revisionism, like when your kids ask you if you took drugs when you were their age, and instead of saying, "Hell yeah! All the time. It was great!" you start to prepare a lecture in your head. Formerly taboo-busting hippies who gleefully welcomed the sexually outrageous *Jiz* and *Snatch Comics* back in the Aquarian Age act embarrassed when they encounter their ilk today. Too many Baby Boomers have matured into the legions of the easily offended. You know, like our parents?

It wasn't just the sex. It was the coupling of unnatural desires with the audacity to disrobe authority. Hell, Republicans and Mormons make billions renting porno films in their hotel chains all across America. They love sexually explicit media—just not when it's combined with satire or sedition.

"It was never about the sex," agreed *Georgia Straight* publisher Dan McLeod, whose Vancouver, British Columbia, underground weekly was busted time after time in the 1970s. "We got fed up with being dragged through the court all the time. They'd always come after

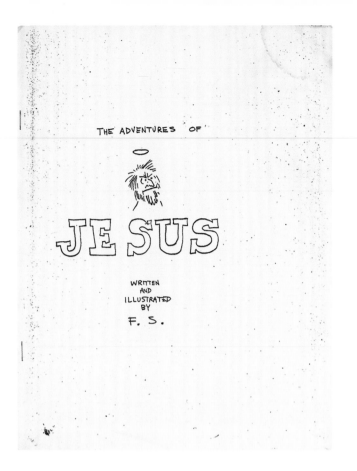

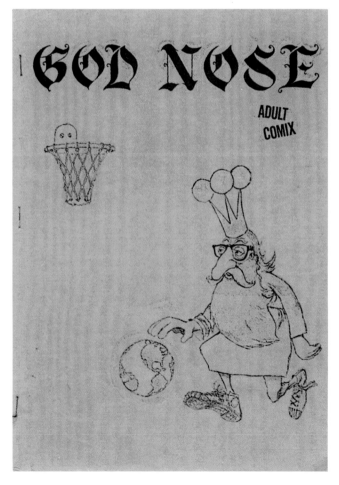

us for the sex charges, but they were just thinly disguised attempts
to suppress our political views. It wasn't sex that was the problem."

Catharsis was often a motivation for comix. Flaunting
fears, shedding demons, confession, confrontation, and revenge
were often behind the creativity. Spain Rodriguez said that
underground comix allowed him to exact his revenge on the
Comics Code Authority, which killed off his favorite E.C. Comics
in 1954. Years later, he found it very satisfying to work his way
through all their restrictions. "It makes me feel good that we made
our blows in the cultural war," said Rodriguez. "We were able
to kick the despicable Comics Code in the teeth. We were able to
make a living. We were able to reflect our times. I think, just like
any industrial process, there's always a lot of waste, but hopefully
there are some gems in all that."

Contenders for the first underground comic book include
The Adventures of Jesus (Frank Stack), *God Nose* (Jack Jackson,
aka "Jaxon"), *Das Kampf* (Vaughn Bode), *The Profit* (Joel Beck),
and *The Surfing Funnies* (Rick Griffin), as well as various fanzines
and humor magazines, but many contend that the real deal
begins with R. Crumb's first issue of *Zap Comix* and that all
these other efforts were just rehearsals. It's like arguing whether
Big Mama Thornton was singing rock 'n' roll or rhythm and
blues. It's about the roots, not the first fruit.

Underground comix sprang up in the convergence of political
repression, psychedelic drugs, the protest movement, and new
innovations in printing technology. The movement was about both
action and reaction—advocating revolution in the streets and
sexual freedom, but also springing from a suburban angst and a
fatalism steeped in atomic bomb drills—drawn in a pictographic
language that reflected the shared rites and customs of American
youth in mid-twentieth century: television, comic books, movies,
and rock 'n' roll.

There was a sense of purpose in creating a new kind of comics,
said Canadian cartoonist Rand Holmes, who worked in relative
isolation from his American colleagues in Vancouver. "It wasn't
the pay. I think mostly I felt I was doing important work. You'd
be right to laugh, but there was magic in the air then, and I really
thought we were going to change the world for the better. Well,
hey, we're all entitled to be young and naïve once in our life."

There was camaraderie aplenty in the early days of the underground press, when spirits were very high, but when the whole
shebang started to wind down a few years later, things became
more competitive. Rival camps of cartoonists took snipes at one
another, gender conflicts divided former friends, royalty checks
arrived late, if at all, and newcomers faced stiff competition for
pages in popular titles.

Would-be underground cartoonists descended on San
Francisco like termites on a tinderbox. By 1972 there were more
than three hundred comics titles in print, but sales were slowing
down. Increased production met declining demand. Bill Griffith
couldn't understand why Print Mint would publish both treasures
and trash without discrimination. "Eclectic would be a kind word
to describe their taste. A cartoonist would come in with a thirty-

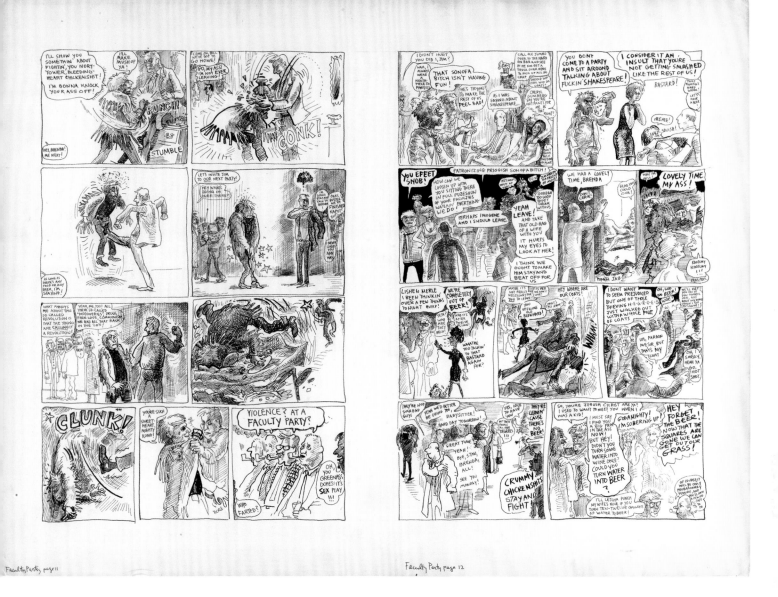

two-page story of their acid trip and they'd publish it, and then next week they'd print the next issue of *Zap* or whatever. They didn't distinguish; they did not discriminate. And for a while that was not a bad economic sense to have, because everything was selling."

For the most part, differences were minor—more a factor of artistic temperament than real enmity, and everybody still got together for a good time at the Rip Off Press parties. For better or worse, they were all in it together. Publishers and distributors traded comic stock with one another, and most cartoonists took their association with the United Comic Workers of America with some degree of seriousness.

Then the triple whammy hit. First Tricky Dick Nixon ended the Vietnam War, and that was the end of the antiwar movement. The president's men then began to systematically dismantle the counterculture by shutting down head shops, infiltrating leftist organizations, reclassifying soft drugs as narcotics, and drawing up enemy lists. In 1973, the Supreme Court's decision in *Miller v. California* that local standards could determine obscenity was the final deathblow to comix.

"Things were never quite that good after Nixon," said Spain Rodriguez. "That whole afterglow of the Summer of Love seemed to last well into the seventies, when there seemed to be a decision at some level to reduce the standard of living of the average American." Good ideas were no longer enough to get a comic off the ground, he said. "When I first got here you could get just about anything published. I had an idea for a comic called *Stomp: The No Nonsense Comic*. I had difficulty getting people to do work for it. I probably could have found someone to publish it. But slowly it became more apparent that underground comix weren't selling as much as they had been. An era had passed."

Underground comix were a flash point on the comic horizon, a moment when the cartoonist's art made a great leap forward, but they also sowed the seeds of their own destruction by choosing to represent rebellion and by rejecting the traditional rewards of the "free market," said Harvey Kurtzman, who published the earliest work of a number of underground cartoonists in *Help!* magazine, though he never shared their antiestablishment philosophy. "The underground was doomed to self-destruction," said Kurtzman. "Like the Shakers who

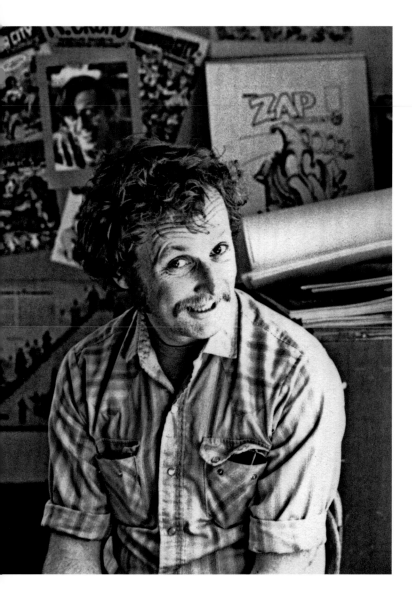

didn't believe in sex, the underground didn't believe in survival. As Gilbert Shelton, the creator of *The Fabulous Furry Freak Brothers* and *Wonder Wart-Hog: The Hog of Steel* put it, 'If we succeed, we've failed. But if we fail, we're successful.' The underground cartoonists had a suicidal philosophy, and the ones I knew were all very frustrated guys, torn between a desire for material success and a contempt for it."

Many of the gains that resulted from this sustained confrontation with the power structure are gone today, hustled off to Homeland Security in a handbasket. Distribution channels are harder to come by, too. In 1968 you could print ten-thousand copies of a sixteen-page tabloid newspaper for a few hundred bucks and ship it off to head shops and record stores across the world. Today, media conglomerates control the popular press and sanitize the troublesome stuff. You can point your blogging finger at the Internet as an example of how to get around the censors, until you think about how many agencies are pawing through your e-mail.

"There was a shaky period there in '70 to '71 where we thought the government was going to clamp down," said Robert Williams. "There was a chance there that the country could have swung to the right. We know for a fact that they were reconditioning internment camps in eastern and southern California. Our phones were being tapped and the cops were watching down the street. It was just continual surveillance. Either we were going to get forced into the army or we'd get thrown into an internment camp. But the third alternative happened, and the whole country loosened up and said 'Fuck the War!' But for three or four years it was a scary situation."

The impact of underground comix affected industry practices as well as social mores. The freedoms, not to mention the profits, flaunted by the San Francisco- and Wisconsin-based comix publishers, forced the New York mainstream boys to loosen up their own pecuniary practices. The example of successful underground publishers like Print Mint, Last Gasp, Rip Off Press, and Kitchen Sink Press has inspired other small outfits to publish the work of artists that they like. Fantagraphics Books, Drawn & Quarterly, Top Shelf Productions, Dark Horse Comics, and others made their mark by targeting specific audiences and addressing their needs. Specialty shops now sell comic books that run the gamut from *X-Men* to X-rated, as well as graphic novels, fantasy gaming cards, and numerous high-priced collectors' goodies, graded and sealed in polypropylene.

"Undergrounds were the first to pay artists on a royalty basis rather than the flat-rate system," said Denis Kitchen. "Royalties treated cartoonists like literary authors and guaranteed them their fair share of the pie. The big publishers traditionally paid the artists a per-page rate regardless of ultimate sales or ancillary benefits to the publisher, a system of obvious inequity. Undergrounds were also the first to recognize the comic creator's right to own the copyright to his or her creation. The generation of upstart cartoonists in my peer group had heard the familiar horror stories about artists being cheated, and we vowed not to let happen to

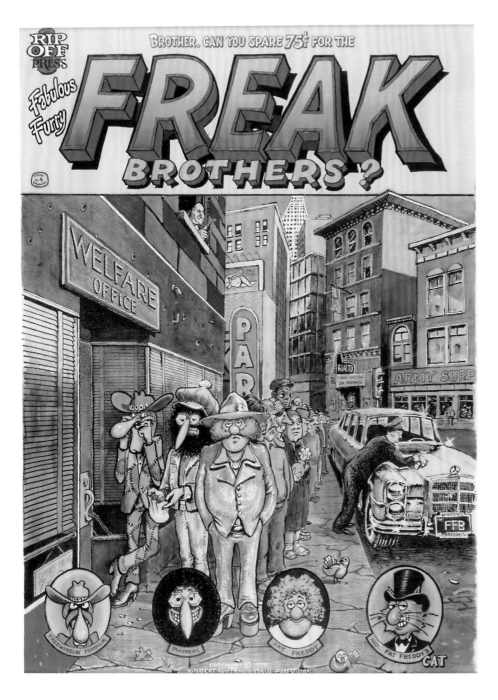

survive the judgments of history than Jasper Johns, Mark di Suvero, or Jim Dine. I hope so. If the best of the comic artists are not perceived as significant artists, I fear that the judgment of history will be that late twentieth-century art was essentially fatuous if not fraudulent."

Comic books are now accepted as educational tools and interpreters of history, animated cartoons are produced for adult audiences, and syndicated cartoonists control their own copyrights. Alternative comics continue to explore untapped territory, and graphic novels are regular fare in bookstores and libraries, but aspirations to art and literature may not save comics from eventually becoming an anachronism, said Art Spiegelman. "It seems to me that comics have already shifted from being an icon of illiteracy to becoming one of our last bastions of literacy. If comics have any problem now, it's that people don't even have the patience to decode them. I don't know if we're the vanguard of another culture or if we're the last blacksmiths."

Even if the efforts of the underground cartoonists bore fruit in countless comic books, it's easy to see why their influence remains subterranean at best. They were harsh, violent, full of drugs and casual sex and calls for revolution. Their wider impact

us what happened to [Superman creators] Jerry Siegel and Joe Shuster, and so many others."

The career choices and artistic avenues available to cartoonists today comprise a much broader spectrum than he found when he was starting out, said Robert Crumb. "The influence of the early underground cartoonists has loosened up comics and broadened the horizons that people saw for comics. That's for certain, but I don't know about the effects on the general population. Probably none. Nobody's ever done a comic that's changed the world, that's for sure."

All of popular media, from movies to music to computer graphics, owes a debt to the pioneering efforts of the underground artists, said *The Adventures of Jesus* creator Frank Stack, now an art professor at the University of Missouri. Fine art also borrows from the vocabulary of cartoons, even in its abstract forms. "It is hard to know if comics of any kind can escape the 'popular-art' ghetto. My own feeling is that Robert Crumb is more likely to

was offset by their blatant disregard for the tender sensibilities of others. Their appeal is to a limited audience—enthusiastic, but finite nonetheless. Underground comix will never be accepted by a mass audience.

Original art is a relative term in comics, because the artwork is created for reproduction, not to be framed and hung on the wall. Comics stories come alive after they've been scanned, stripped, printed, bound, trimmed, and shipped out in trucks. What ultimately counts is how the work looks in print. Original pages are often unsightly, with scribbles on the margins, gobs of Wite-Out, stains, and dried-up Zip-A-Tone, but some boards are as perfect as any museum piece, penciled and inked with consummate skill, and show even greater detail than the printed version. When you read a comic book you can get lost in the story and forget the storyteller, but when you look at a masterful piece of comic art, you are acutely aware of its creator.

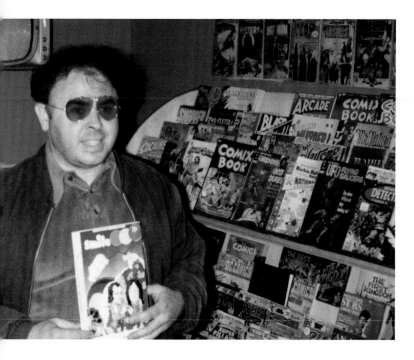

"IT WAS A LOOSE COMMUNITY of artists devoted to revitalizing a humble art form, though not all spirits were kindred," said Justin Green. "Like any movement, there were cliques and warring factions, but all held to the ideal of reaching a common audience while reinventing the formal boundaries that had defined the medium."

THE *ZAP* COLLECTIVE

Robert Crumb drew the first *Zap Comix* by himself, but within a year Rick Griffin, Victor Moscoso, S. Clay Wilson, Gilbert Shelton, Spain Rodriguez, and Robert Williams joined him in the *Zap* Collective. "Why split the pie any further?" asked S. Clay Wilson. "Kind of like an art mafia."

E.C. REVIVALISTS: HORROR AND SCIENCE FICTION

Gary Arlington, whose San Francisco Comic Book Company was the ground zero of underground comix, was the inspiration behind *Skull Comics* and *Slow Death,* which featured fantasy tales of horror and cosmic retribution, as well as the real-life terrors of overpopulation and ecological catastrophe. Regular contributors included Greg Irons, Jack Jackson, Rory Hayes, Jim Osborne, Dave Sheridan, and Richard Corben.

FUNNY HIPPY DOPE STORIES

Gilbert Shelton practically owned this genre, with his fabulously successful *Furry Freak Brothers*. When *FFB* comics began to sell faster than he could draw them, Shelton enlisted the help of cartoonists Dave Sheridan and Paul Mavrides to keep the continuing adventures rolling along. Rand Holmes gave a different spin to counterculture slapstick with *The Adventures of Harold Hedd,* who was an inventor, carpenter, pilot, musician, and also handy with firearms.

SATIRISTS AND INTELLECTUALS

Young Lust, Zippy the Pinhead, Short Order Comics and, later, *Arcade* magazine showcased the literary and satirical comic art that represented this art faction, which included work by Kim Deitch, Roger Brand, Jay Kinney, Justin Green, Willy Murphy, Jim Osborne, Art Spiegelman, and Bill Griffith.

THE AIR PIRATES

The Air Pirates were noteworthy for bringing sexual liberation to the Walt Disney stable of funny animals. Ted Richards, Bobby London, Gary Hallgren, and Shary Flenniken learned the fine art of cartooning by copying the styles of old comic masters under the guidance of syndicated cartoonist Dan O'Neill.

WOMEN'S LIBERATION

Underground comix was mainly a boy's club, but Trina Robbins edited the first all-women comic book, *It Ain't Me Babe,* published by Last Gasp Funnies in 1971. Its success soon led to other women's titles, included *Wimmen's Comix, Tits N' Clits,* and *All*

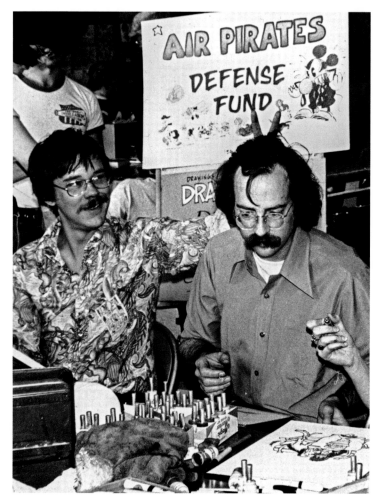

TOP | GARY ARLINGTON
An early retailer, publisher, and promoter of underground comix, Arlington holds a copy of *Smile* no. 1 at his San Francisco Comic Book Company shop, 1976

BOTTOM | GARY HALLGREN AND DAN O'NEILL
attend an Air Pirates benefit signing at the Berkeley Con, April 1973

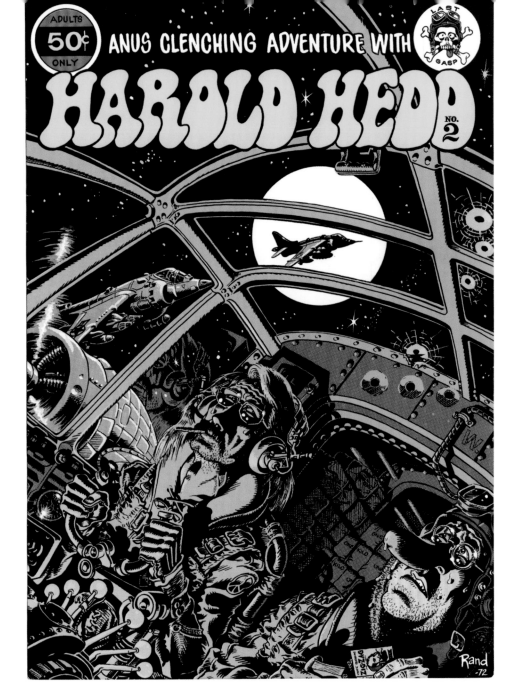

ADULTS ONLY 50¢

ANUS CLENCHING ADVENTURE WITH

HAROLD HEDD NO. 2

LAST GASP

LEFT | RAND HOLMES
Harold Hedd no. 2, cover, 1972

BOTTOM | L TO R: DON GLASSFORD,
DENIS KITCHEN, ROBERT CRUMB,
SKIP WILLIAMSON, AND JAY LYNCH
Milwaukee, April 15, 1971
This photo was taken the day this crew
and others drew the "Let's Be Realistic
Comics" jam pages. *The Arms of Krupp*,
held by Jay Lynch, was an in-joke (the
book served as the inspiration for
Krupp Comic Works' name).

Girl Thrills. Contributors included Willy Mendes, Michele Brand, Aline Kominsky, Diane Noomin, and Dori Seda.

BIJOU PUBLISHING EMPIRE

Bijou Funnies publisher/cartoonist Jay Lynch appointed himself the publicist of underground comix to spread the word and put people together. *Bijou*'s contributors included Lynch, Skip Williamson, Robert Crumb, Art Spiegelman, Justin Green, Jay Kinney, and Kim Deitch.

KRUPP COMIC WORKS

Krupp Comic Works, which later became Kitchen Sink Press, was a distinct departure from what publisher/cartoonist Denis Kitchen called the "West Coast slop-and-drip school of cartooning." First-generation Krupp cartoonists Don Glassford, Wendel Pugh, Jim Mitchell, and Howard Cruse appeared in titles like *Mom's Homemade Comics*, *Smile*, and *Barefootz Funnies*. In time, however, Krupp dipped into the cesspool of depravity with titles like *Bizarre Sex* and *Dope Comix*. ■

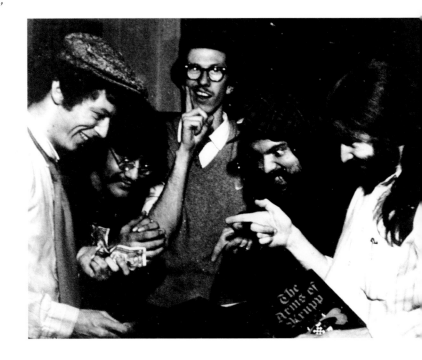

50¢
LAST GASP
IT AINT ME BABE
WOMENS LIBERATION
Trina

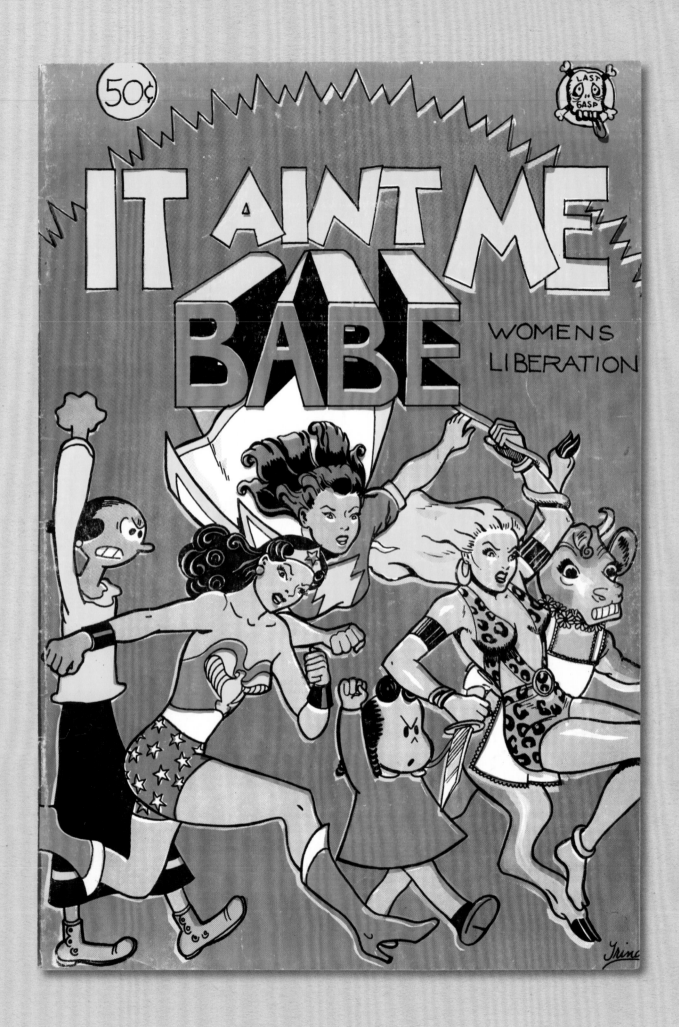

Wimmen's Studies
By Trina Robbins

IN 1970S SAN FRANCISCO, BIRTHPLACE OF the underground comix movement, the comix scene was more than merely a boys' club. In part reacting against the repressive mainstream Comics Code, in part following the hippie dogma to "let it all hang out," and definitely influenced by the misogynist comix of counterculture hero Robert Crumb, in most San Francisco comix circles it was almost de rigueur for male underground cartoonists to include violence against women in their comix, and to portray this violence as humor. To these guys, and to their many male readers, graphic rape scenes were boffo—beheaded women had them rolling in the aisles.

Women who thought panels of rape, torture, and murder were not funny were often told by men that they simply had no sense of humor. To many male underground cartoonists, criticism of Crumb was heresy. Such attitudes did not help get the only two women underground cartoonists in San Francisco invited into most of the guys' books.

This was the situation to which I responded in 1970 by joining the staff of *It Ain't Me Babe*, one of the first women's liberation newspapers in the country, and with their moral support, putting together the very first all-woman comic book, *It Ain't Me Babe* comics. It wasn't easy finding women cartoonists in 1970. Willy Mendes, the only other San Francisco woman cartoonist, contributed an eight-page story and the back cover. I contributed two stories and the front cover. Socialist cartoonist Lisa Lyons contributed some beautifully drawn pages about the revolution, and the *It Ain't Me Babe* newspaper staff produced a collectively written-and-drawn comic in which Petunia Pig, Little Lulu, Betty, and Veronica join Supergirl in a consciousness-raising group.

By 1972, I had already published my own comic book, *Girl Fight*, and, together with Mendes, put together *All Girl Thrills*, while Mendes had published her own book, *Illuminations*. *It Ain't Me Babe*, the book that started it all, had done well enough that publisher Ron Turner,

OPPOSITE | TRINA ROBBINS
It Ain't Me Babe, cover, 1970

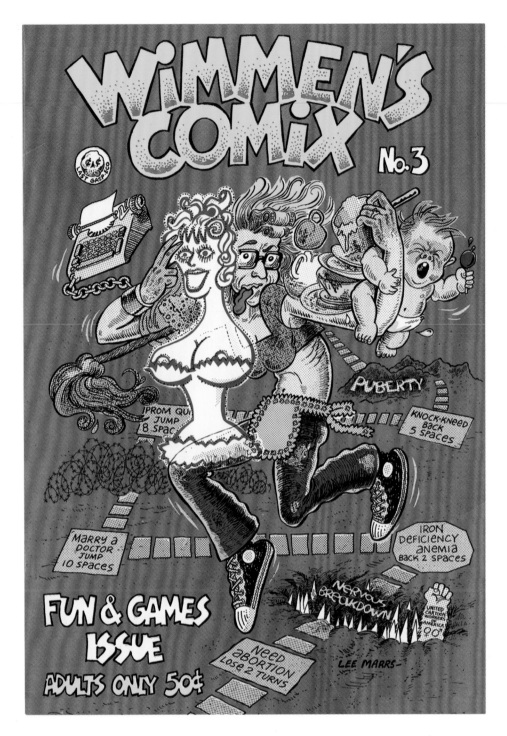

ABOVE | LEE MARRS
Wimmen's Comix no. 3, cover, 1973

OPPOSITE | JOYCE FARMER
Tits & Clits Comix no. 6, cover, 1980

of Last Gasp, wanted to publish a second book. However, I had been dissatisfied with the quality of *It Ain't Me Babe*, and didn't want to produce another issue.

Patti Moodian, working at Last Gasp, learned of Turner's desire to publish a women's liberation title and called together nine other women (the "founding mothers") for a meeting at her house. Of the original founding mothers, Lee Marrs was the most experienced, having assisted newspaper cartoonist Tex Blaisdell on his strip *Little Orphan Annie* and contributed gags to Mort Walker's strip *Hi and Lois*. In 1971, along with Mal Warwick, she had formed the Alternative Features Syndicate (AFS) to distribute news, features, and comics to college and underground papers. She was already working on her first solo book, *Pudge, Girl Blimp*, which would not see print for another two years.

Another founding mother, Sharon Rudahl, had drawn political comics for the Madison, Wisconsin, underground paper *Takeover*, and was now living in the San Francisco Good Times commune and working on their underground paper.

Perhaps because of our political backgrounds or perhaps simply because we were women, the Women's Comix Collective's methods differed from those of the male underground from the start. In a 1979 interview in *Cultural Correspondence* magazine, founding mother Terre Richards says:

> We…decided that…we would function as a collective, a term rather loosely used in those days to mean there would be no leader

or editor, but instead a rotating editorship, with everyone contributing their energy to the paperwork and general supportiveness of the group.

It took us three meetings to settle on a name. While coming up with such bizarre suggestions as *Queen Kong*, we kept repeating, "What shall we call this women's comic?" Finally we realized that we had known its name all along, and thus, with a small spelling change, was born *Wimmen's Comix*.

From the first issue, we drew on our own personal experiences and those of other women. We tackled subjects that the guys wouldn't touch with a ten-foot pole—subjects such as abortion, lesbianism, menstruation, and childhood sexual abuse. Aline Kominsky produced what was probably the first autobiographical comic, a subject that is still in vogue today among women cartoonists; I drew the first comic about a lesbian.

In a strange case of California synchronicity, although the founding mothers didn't know it at the time, two Southern California women, Joyce Farmer and Lynn Chevely (under the pseudonym Chin Lively), were reacting to the sexism they found in male-oriented underground comix by producing their own title, *Tits & Clits Comix*. Although *Wimmen's Comix* is generally thought to be the first women's underground title, Farmer's and Chevely's book actually arrived on newsstands two months before *Wimmen's*.

The first few issues of *Wimmen's* were uneven, as so many contributors had much to learn about drawing comics. I sometimes despaired that the book would remain a kind of lady's auxiliary, because many contributors were wives or girlfriends of male cartoonists, but as cream rises to the top, less talented contributors dropped out and better artists emerged. Highly regarded cartoonists Melinda Gebbie (*Lost Girls*) and Roberta Gregory (*Naughty Bits*) both drew their first comics for *Wimmen's* in 1973 and 1974, respectively. Later issues published work by Phoebe Gloeckner, Shary Flenniken, Dori Seda, Krystine Kryttre, and Lynda Barry. Farmer and Chevely contributed to our books, and we contributed to theirs.

It was not always smooth sailing. Lesbians accused us of heterosexism. We were criticized for being an all-white group, but during the entire twenty-year run of *Wimmen's*, we never received one submission from an African-American woman cartoonist. *Ms.* magazine refused to accept our ads. In 1973 we received hate mail accusing us of being FBI informants or, as the letter writer put it, "crewcut she-pricks." Of course there were fights. Because of disagreements with the editors, I dropped out of two issues, but I returned for the next.

Our libertarian publisher didn't make judgments, but at a certain point we started feeling uncomfortable about being included with such comics as *Horny Biker Sluts*, and we looked for a new publisher. In fact, we went through two new publishers, each one selling fewer and fewer numbers, before we decided to call it quits.

Wimmen's Comix had sold well back in the days of head shops, but the head shops closed and the only place to find comics was comic book stores, owned or managed by super hero fans who preferred to sell super hero comics to other super hero fans and

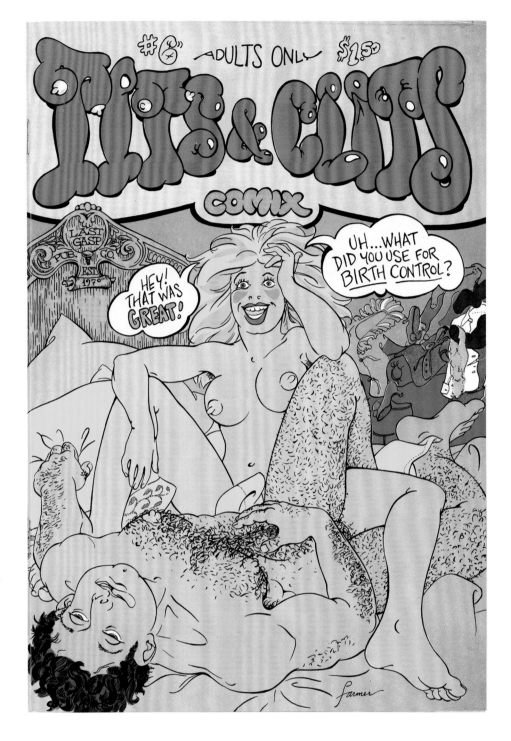

who understocked, or simply didn't carry, "chick books." Caryn Leschen, editor of the last issue, expressed our feelings when she wrote in her editorial:

> The print run was too small and all the stores, as usual, will sell out, but they won't reorder because "Women don't buy comics." Bullshit. How did they sell out in the first place?

Wimmen's Comix finally folded in 1992. By that time there were more women creating comics than ever before. They self-published or were published by small presses. They were already beginning to put their comics up on websites on the Internet. *Wimmen's Comix* opened the door for them all—and the door is still open. ∎

MICKEY MOUSE
MEETS THE
AIR PIRATES
Funnies
NIX KIDS-
ADULTS ONLY!
#1
50¢

The Undergrounds
By Paul Buhle

ow to Pray the Rosary

Glory Be

Mystery
Our
er

10 Hail Marys

3rd Mystery
and Our Father

Glory Be

10
Hail
Marys

10
Hail
Marys

5th Mystery
and
Our Father

2nd Mystery
and
Our Father

Glory
Be

10
Hail
Marys

Glory
Be

10
Hail
Marys

1st Mystery and
Our Father

Hail
Holy Queen

Glory Be

3 Hail Marys

1 Our Father

Sign of the Cross
and Apostles' Creed

ROSARY is a form of vocal and mental prayer on the
teries of our Redemption, divided into twenty decades.

recitation of each decade is accompanied by meditation on
of the twenty events or "mysteries."

Mysteries consist of 4 groups pictured on pages 2, 3, 4 & 5.

F AMERICAN COMICS traveling exhibition of 2005–06
e have arguably placed the story of American comic art in a
a half century late in arriving, but no less welcome for that
ts of a formidable group of artists in what is likely the most
bloid and comic book) have been treated as something better
t scene or a source of interest mainly to overgrown juveniles
rstwhile underground comix giants Art Spiegelman and
ifteen masters chosen, as was their great inspiration, Harvey
ken devotees of the underground, Gary Panter and Chris
of ten other classicists so that, in all, "underground" cartoon-
n list.
s arbitrary, places our subject well: Underground comix,
stablished in the new comics art pantheon. This pantheon
sible foothold within the American publishing scene: For
thetic ones, the graphic novel has most decidedly arrived in
here to stay—the next "new thing" in publishing history.
comic book is also increasingly seen as a source of nonfiction
history-telling. Historians, for their part, like so many other scholarly observers, seem at
once bemused and a bit puzzled at the meteoric rise of comics and the space they now take
up not only in the bookstores but also in the neighborhood library, where whole rooms have
been cleared out of the old stock for picture books. The full story is no doubt alarming to
old-style professors viewing with horror the replacement of scholarly prose with images
and dialogue. But comics, once more highly regarded in Europe and Asia than in America
as a format for artistic expression, have also begun to invade even the academic world, as

OPPOSITE | BOBBY LONDON
Air Pirates Funnies no. 1, cover, 1971

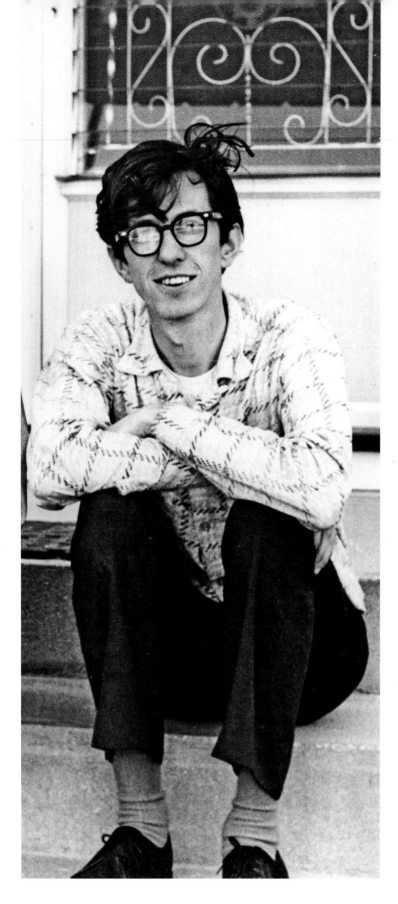

they reach the classroom and the ordinary reader, especially the young reader (and even the occasional sympathetic professor).

Somehow, however, the full significance of the underground comix movement seems to have slipped from view. To offer a contrast: Any avant-garde and famous (or infamous) school of painting inevitably fades during the rise of the next wave, but the work of the original remains in public and private collections, becomes one more building block for classroom discussion and erudite analysis for art historians, and so on. Cubism, Futurism, Dadaism, Surrealism, Abstract Expressionism—even the versions of Socialist Realism that found their best expression on the walls of public buildings thanks to the New Deal's Public Works Administration—have all shared this fate. But when the infrastructure of the undergrounds collapsed thirty years ago, after a brief rush of production, their very history seemed threatened along with their existence. Of the several dozen talented artists appearing regularly in print during the early 1970s, only a handful ever made as much as a low-rent living from the work, and not surprisingly, most of them had dropped from sight by the Reagan years.

The underground press has had an afterlife of sorts in the so-called alternative press, and likewise the underground comix in alternative comics. Selected work of some of that same handful of underground artists found a home here, as did selections from their mainstream precursors (in some cases, heavy influences), from Winsor McCay to Al Capp. Thanks to successful legal efforts, repression of sexual images that had first been displayed in the undergrounds (apart, that is, from the Tijuana Bibles, under-the-counter pornographic comics produced in the United States from the 1920s until the early 1960s) was mostly held at bay. It was an important development and made some of the most intriguing underground materials available to new generations of artists and readers. And yet, despite the fact that, in the new century, R. Crumb's originals fetch large prices and artists beyond the mainstream can congratulate themselves on past Pulitzers and MacArthur "genius" awards (actually, only two underground artists: Spiegelman and Ben Katchor, respectively), the real history of the art explosion during the late 1960s and early 1970s remains practically terra incognita. Notwithstanding the appearance of several popular histories, only the scholar or dedicated fan would know of the distinct significance of the period for comic art.

It has often seemed that, like the counterculture years at large, underground comix have come to occupy a dreamlike space in American life and art, scarcely understood at the time, more mythicized or repressed (sometimes both simultaneously) than appreciated. Still, even if the names of artists beyond Crumb, Spiegelman, and Bill Griffith (we should add Harvey Pekar, whose *American Splendor* appeared at the very end of the early wave in 1976, and whose status was secured by the 2003 film of the same title) are the only ones likely to be recognized by the casual reader, the imprint of the movement's stylistic breakthrough remains. The astonishingly sudden emancipation of artistic expression, from music to marijuana, realized in the most vernacular genres of print, has survived in collective memory. One could even argue that later popular culture has retained modes of the 1960s in ways that only the Golden Age of Hollywood (conducted for the most part under the tightest artistic censorship) can rival. For our purposes, it also marked an artistic development of a most unique kind: the fusion of popular art and avant-garde, even academic avant-garde art buried in a deeper history.

It probably helps to look back historically from what is now an appreciable distance. Seen afresh among those booming 1960s genres, "comix" (the very name belongs to the 1960s, appearing and disappearing within a decade) retain something unique, something that belongs to the history of the yellow press and the lowly comic book alike, the appearance of local tabloids unbidden by any corporate influence, the small-scale commerce of the head shop. In short, a slice of life considerably more grassroots than any other artistic genre of the time, and for that very reason, more vulnerable. The comix scene, unlike rock music, had no *Rolling Stone* to promote its personalities and salability, nor a radio playlist or mega-concerts, just the hand-to-hand (and hand-to-mouth) trade of aroused and passing interest.

This time-centeredness gives special pause now, for several unique reasons. Another failed project of Empire—a monstrously misguided and botched military adventure far from native shores—has brought back the dark side of the 1960s. The antiwar comics of the (mostly) younger artists of *World War 3 Illustrated* look more like the antiwar comics of the 1960s and early 1970s than anything seen in more than thirty years. It can't be an accident. The vivid new interest among thousands of young people in the history of that time, those years long-cursed by conservatives, neoconservatives, and many species of liberals as a source of civilization's inner dangers, seem to have come home to roost.

Underground comix not only epitomize the fabled 1960s— more precisely beginning in the second half of that decade and running into the first half of the 1970s—but more to the point here, visualize them. They simultaneously mark the passage of American art from the Abstract Expressionism of the early Cold War years to a re-figuration (that is, recuperation of the human figure within art), but with the experimentation of the abstractionists largely intact or, rather, appropriately internalized. It takes little away from Andy Warhol or Roy Lichtenstein to note that Crumb and Spiegelman have assembled, across their careers, more significant work, drawing more deeply from some of the same sources in popular culture and making more sense of what they discovered for themselves. Or that editor/artist Trina

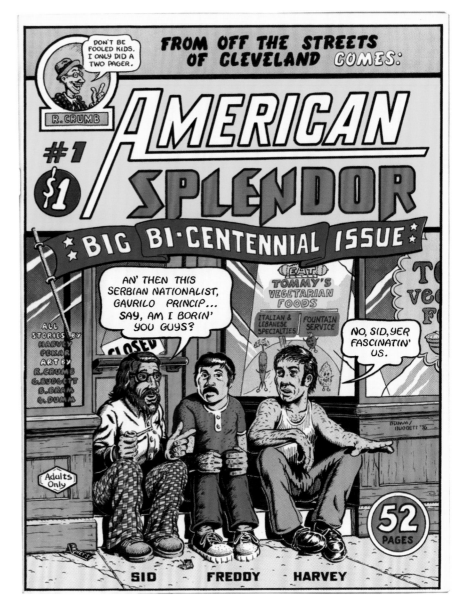

Robbins has probably added as much to re-figuration as, say, Alice Neel, in the sense that Robbins's example, mentorship, and encouragement have successfully brought several generations of women artists into publishable projects. The exhibit upon which this book is based clearly argues that underground comix must, by now, become part of art history.

Any such history would do well to begin with a detailed examination of the underground's influences, with Harvey Kurtzman's *MAD* perhaps being the most widely acknowledged antecedent. The story of *MAD* and its influence on the generation of 1960s artists is told in several places in this volume, and more explicitly within the captions of pieces displayed. Some deep influences should nevertheless be noted in passing as the background for any introduction to the undergrounds.

MAD arose at the final glorious moment of comic books' maturation, when the E.C. mini-empire lifted comics art to an unprecedented level. *MAD* magazine evolved from *MAD* comics not only because of the repression of the comics genre (and the growing competition of television), but also because Kurtzman and publisher William M. Gaines had worked out the next step in magazine production.

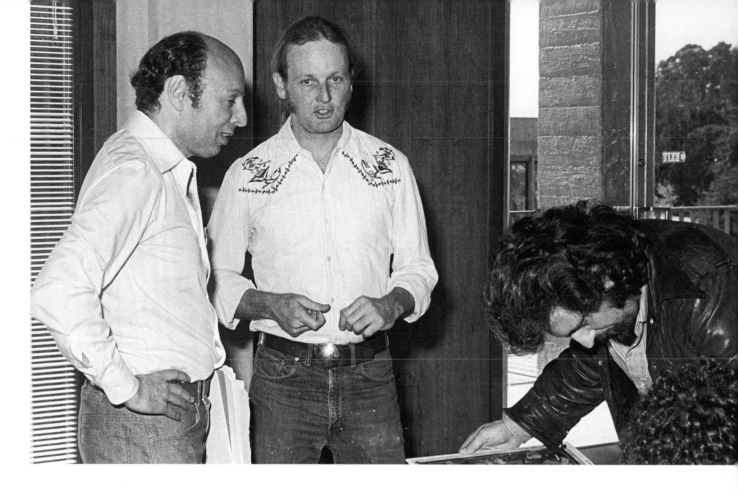

The successive financial failures of editor Harvey Kurtzman after *MAD* were coded in the limitations of print technology and contemporary newsstand sales, as Kurtzman sought to repeat *MAD*'s success. *Trump, Humbug,* and *Help!* were undercapitalized, and none of them really had the chance to find its audience or even to pay the creative staff properly, but technological advances afoot would soon allow short runs of tabloids at low production prices. This possibility would not likely have interested Kurtzman himself, locked into a commercial magazine-and-newsstand circuit. Underground newspapers, however, by reaching out to an audience and creating one in the process, made the most of the fresh technology, and the comix really started here. Moreover, what would have been banned just a few years earlier now came in under the radar, distributed outside official and even respectable channels. This heralded a new phase of print history.

The abandonment of *MAD* comics also left behind what Kurtzman fondly remembered as the "old German craftsmen," the printers who produced the color plates with skills that were doomed to become outmoded. One might say that these German-Americans, pride of the printing trade (Kurtzman's own father was a printer), were the last of a breed centuries old. The prestige of the oil painters whose works are displayed upon museum walls serves to disguise the deeper reality of the largely anonymous working artist and his (or her) relationship with an equally anonymous but ever-expanding public. Accelerating industrialization, as a certain German philosopher and economist suggested, creates a seller for the buyer as well as a buyer for the seller. The comic strip, born near the end of the nineteenth century within the folds of the dominant media

of the day, became the result. So was the comic book of the late 1930s onward, and no less was the underground comic of the late 1960s. The comix artist in a makeshift studio was the ever-so-great grandchild of those artisans producing book illustrations, sharing with them economic compulsions and artistic idiosyncrasies often more spontaneous than planned.

The issues of technique tend to be lost here, as in all areas of popular art. An assumption of style as merely stamped-on, almost meaningless, is thought to be the just deserts of the mass mind and the newspaper or comic publisher. The assumption is by no means entirely mistaken from the standpoint of the entrepreneur. As Kurtzman once observed, despairingly, the comic book publisher was usually an accountant who viewed the artist as the most expendable part of the enterprise. But the standpoint of the artist could be different when the message of artistic worthlessness had been rejected, which is to say, had not been internalized as emblematic of personal failure.

Kurtzman described the alternative to style being relegated to an afterthought, for him, as the romance of the brushstroke. If the heart of the comic narrative is the idea (something the hacks disregarded), the technique of the brush was the living expression of that idea, not separate from the idea but organically connected to it. As a foremost social critic in a medium where social criticism had been least expected, Kurtzman was nevertheless drawn to artistic detail. His major artistic collaborator, Will Elder—arguably the most immediate precursor for the underground artists—extended Kurtzman's thought and his brushstrokes into an infinitely complex visual reality.

To return to the market: The fact that the undergrounds' immediate and somewhat more distant precursors had mainly sprung up in any number of sites, but notably the Bay Area and Austin, Texas, rather than Manhattan (and when there, the East Village rather than uptown), speaks volumes. These were counterculture havens before "counterculture" had become a telling term. Chicago, even in its considerable glory, had always been a publishing second city. San Francisco, with City Lights Books, added something dramatically new and different to American culture, no less by the defiance of existing censorship laws (City Lights' successful court case in 1957 against the suppression of Allen Ginsberg's *Howl and Other Poems*) than by the freshness, openness, Western-ness of expression. Across the Bay a few years later, Joel Beck was a Berkeley personality as well as an eccentric self-publisher. One might add that music-store clerk Philip K. Dick set his cap in the direction of the pulp press for his genius radical fiction. Meanwhile, Gilbert Shelton had a happy home in the University of Texas's popular satire magazine, *The Texas Ranger*, before the birth of the countercultural *Rag*. Kurtzman was to say later that when he originally launched *MAD*, he was reading college satire magazines heavily, scattered across the map. They had grassroots verve to spare.

Shelton's *Feds 'N' Heads* of 1968 was, even more than Beck's *Lenny of Laredo* (a 1966 satire on Lenny Bruce), really the first of the new genre. Independently published and self-enclosed, it showcased Wonder Wart-Hog, the satirical antihero who might be called the son of *MAD* comics' hapless Clark Bent. This time, he was close to both the Hells Angels and Janis Joplin (a personal friend of the artist), all of a piece with freewheeling Austin, where Shelton sketched a world of images.

The nature of his Fabulous Furry Freak Brothers, the first fully developed protagonists of the undergrounds (at least, the first group of them), was the chief source of the interest in Fat Freddy, Freewheelin' Frank, and Phineas. That is, dope. There was also sex (at this point implied off-panel rather than shown vividly), anti-cop narratives, and *MAD*-style satires of advertising. But marijuana and LSD were the manna that could alter a vision of society, perhaps work wonders on Middle America.

We need to go sideways and backward from this narrative because, of course, Shelton was hardly alone, just ahead of his time in publishing a comic whose cover included the half-ironic warning, "For Enlightened Adults Only!" Half a dozen other future comix artists had been publishing commercially since the early 1960s. To take two cases in point: Rick Griffin (who would later do the title page of the Shelton-edited *Radical America Komiks*) had for years made a living drawing illustrations for surfer publications, and Robert Williams had been producing art for LA-based hot-rod magazines. Several other artists—Roger Brand was an assistant to DC's Gil Kane (of *Green Lantern* fame)—had been working on the fringes of the East Coast comic book/pulp mainstream. A small handful, including a teenage Crumb, had published their own little fanzine-like comics for small-scale, noncommercial distribution. Useful experiments, one and all.

Then came the underground tabloids, among them such early entrants as the *East Village Other*, the *Los Angeles Free Press*,

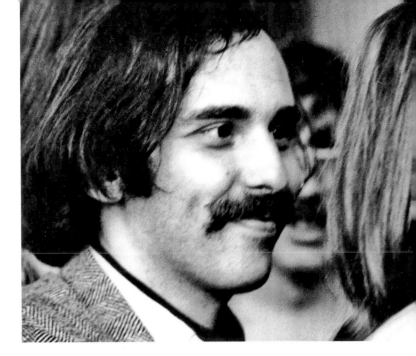

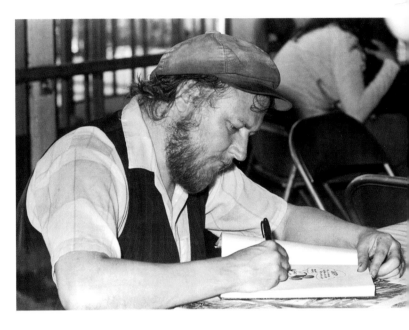

OPPOSITE | HARVEY KURTZMAN, GILBERT SHELTON, and SPAIN RODRIGUEZ
Berkeley Con, April 1973

TOP | ART SPIEGELMAN
Berkeley Con, April 1973

BOTTOM | JOEL BECK
Berkeley Con, April 1973

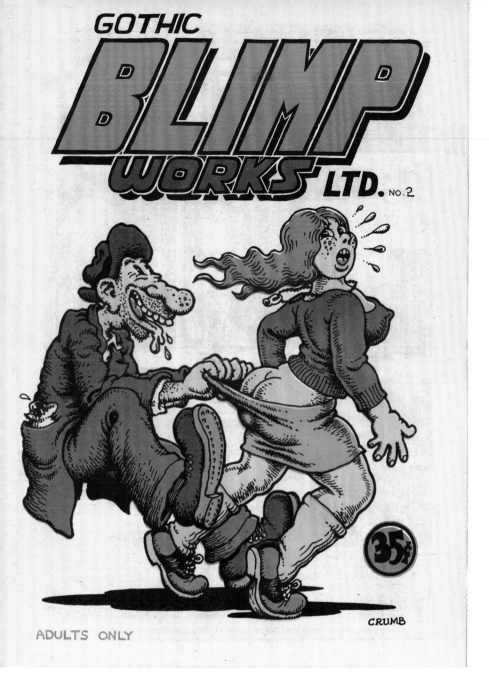

GOTHIC BLIMP WORKS LTD. NO. 2

ADULTS ONLY

CRUMB

ABOVE | ROBERT CRUMB,
Gothic Blimp Works Ltd. no. 2, cover, 1969

OPPOSITE TOP | GILBERT SHELTON,
Feds 'N' Heads, cover, 1968

OPPOSITE BOTTOM | ROBERT CRUMB,
Yellow Dog, vol. 1 no. 1, cover, 1968

and three all-comix outlets: *Gothic Blimp Works* (New York), *Yarrowstalks* (Philadelphia), and *Yellow Dog* (Berkeley). Now the artists had a real audience, if hardly a paying one, growing by leaps and bounds with each new underground paper that offered a comix page (and nearly all of them did). What they lacked was a Greenwich-Village-of-the-1910s-like artistic center. This time, it happened to be San Francisco.

This geopolitical development could not have been predicted. Powerful daily newspapers had long existed far from New York, but the book-publishing industry (including comic books and pulp magazines), had never strayed much farther than Connecticut. We have so far mainly interviews, and a bit of historical journalism, devoted to the emerging publishers of the comix, above all Don Schenker of Apex Novelties in Berkeley, or to Schenker's friendly competition, especially Rip Off Press, Inc. But the records would surely reveal the frantic combination of talent, energy, dope, and almost hand-to-hand distribution during the first years in particular. Other comix publishers who followed shortly, including Denis Kitchen's brainchild, Kitchen Sink Press in Milwaukee, each built upon these curious foundations.

The marvel of it all is that suddenly, almost anything seemed possible. From the beginning, a requisite dose of sex would be sure to add to sales. Most artists, male and female alike, had long wanted to work with a sexual content hitherto forbidden. "Sex sells," a standard formula for the pulps (as well as Hollywood, television, advertising, and so on), was also an invitation to testosterone-laden narratives, not just "sexist" but often violent and sometimes cruel. When Trina Robbins complained in later years that the overdose of sexist sex had killed the undergrounds, she exaggerated, although the comix clearly could have used a lot more feminist sex—of the type realized in *It Ain't Me Babe* and the over-the-top *Tits & Clits*—from the beginning. Familiar, barely satirical, un-reflexive male fantasies quickly became repetitive, while feminist sex fantasies and the small genre of gay and lesbian comix had barely gotten under way when the comix crashed.

But we are getting ahead of our story, because the sheer variety of the art and its placement within youth culture (or counterculture), as well as the general sentiment against the war, the draft, racism, environmental devastation, and just plain corporate capitalism, were decisive influences, as were the commercial or noncommercial repackaging of sex for mutual pleasure. These dissident themes alone would have placed the undergrounds within the key rebellious artistic traditions of the American twentieth century.

Underground comix deftly united the most vernacular of all arts, the comic book, with political rebellion and a reflective critique of American culture. To the staid traditions of nineteenth-century American easel art, the 1913 Armory Show and work in the *Masses* magazine (1911–17) had provided equal shocks. Abstraction, and a close view of life in the streets, only produced a modest revolution in American high art, because the new Museum of Modern Art didn't have the following that its European counterparts possessed for a class of the intelligentsia. No doubt also because the most potentially rewarding of modern art forms—Dada, in tune with the scraps of popular culture that made the U.S. dynamic—had faded early, with the retreat of the revolutionary waves.

But the logic of Ash Can Art offered a keen glimpse at what and where the comix would be one day. Politically radical Expressionism, militant lithographs, the cartoons of the *New Masses* (Communist-leaning successor to the *Masses*), and a unique genre of popularly available lithographs were part of a wave of political art larger than the *Masses* milieu had been. Government support and the spirit of New Deal anti-fascism/social reconstruction had supplied the legitimacy that no radical art before or after was likely to achieve. Their vogue was destined to pass yet more quickly, thanks to the Cold War's impact. The Works Progress Administration murals remained on walls of public institutions, a frozen memory of the attempt to bring together the popularly accessible memory with some of the best of American artwork—until the overpowering triumph of Abstract Expressionism and its corporate and government public relations machine.

The story is somewhat more complicated in the world of the vernacular, as is nearly always the case beneath the radar of the critic/gatekeepers. Artists in the mainstream Yiddish press had drawn for the left-wing press, usually under assumed names, and a small handful of artists adopted the same technique with comics industry day jobs and their art for the Communists' *Daily Worker*. (A teenage Harvey Kurtzman himself drew backgrounds for one of the *Worker*'s comic strip artists.) Few wider left-wing influences could be detected in the mostly superpatriotic comic books until the rise of E.C.'s socially critical lines. *MAD* comics constituted practically the only example of abstraction (and more to the point, premature Postmodernism) of the contemporary comics art world. But it may have been said to have planted the seed—just as the Congressional investigations forced *MAD* into magazine format—for a different way to look at art, and not just comics art.

Because his own influences lay as much in Marvel and in painting as in comics, Ben Katchor, one of the major ambiguous successors to the artists of the underground, has suggested that the trends of the late 1960s and 1970s could be laid in part to the re-figuration of art, the return of the human figure. Pop Art was only the most visible, media-treated element of a rebellion from Abstraction. A "New York" artist like Larry Rivers, in satires of American patriotic icons and his use of improbable mundane materials, was already, in the later 1950s, a half step toward

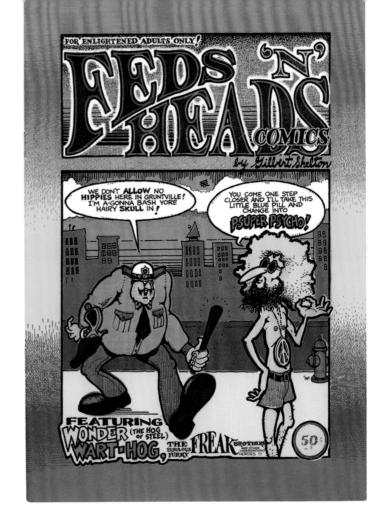

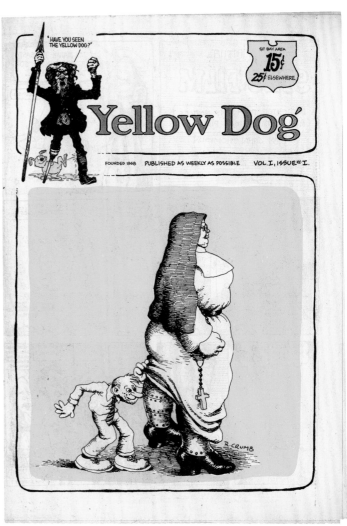

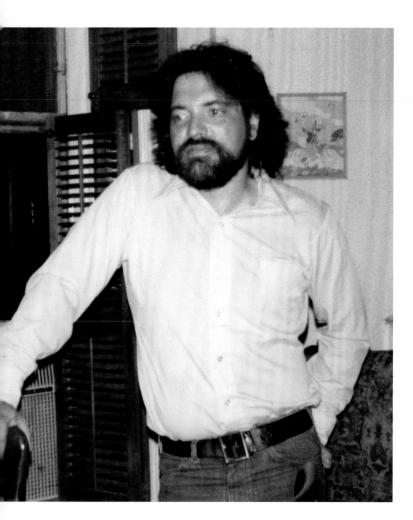

somewhere in the middle ground, able to tell a one-page story rather like a stand-up routine centered on a single joke. Over a period of a few years, talented and radical storytellers like Spain Rodriguez could develop substantive historical narratives, even whole comics, while artists like Crumb drew profusely but with stories of several pages broken up by one-page or less riffs. Griffith and Jay Kinney teamed up to produce *Young Lust*, the longest-running series of comics made up of stories, a satire on romance comics that outlasted the original and encouraged artists to come a bit closer to the standard comic book format.

Beyond the quick thrills of sex and other transgressive acts made visual and usually funny (or at least satirical), the attempt to realize an LSD vision, originally launched for rock posters, offered a striking innovation that may be said to have borrowed from Pop Art, but brought it to a new conclusion. Moscoso, who sampled Disney, and John Thompson, who drew upon Eastern religion, clearly needed no texts for their messages, or they used words in nonlinear ways, as did Buckwheat Florida, Jr., and Andy Martin, who drew from no known sources. Robert Williams and Rick Griffin, working closer to comic traditions, moved far beyond earlier limits. Felix the Cat had walked on lightning and Walt Kelly's *Pogo* had its near-psychedelic moments, but undergrounders quickly reached somewhere comics had not gone, with a leap not likely to be made again.

It was a once-in-a-century opportunity for art, before Postmodernism, to embrace both the vernacular (memories of popular icons) and the infinite (seen more often than not in an ironic fashion). As intimately urban-ethnic as Crumb's spectacular work would remain (or return to), it was always the 1920s–40s images on acid, a combination that others might hint at or sample but that remained classic Crumb.

A second definitely related and widely misunderstood impulse might be called religious but would better be described as spiritual, naturally including LSD "kozmik trooths" (Crumb's phrase)—but also much, much more. A good fifteen years before the emergence of Liberation Theology, the notion of a radical Christology was rare, although the college professor (Frank Stack) who called himself Foolbert Sturgeon did some wonderful "what if Jesus returned" strips in *The Adventures of Jesus*. But that did not mean that religious rumination, beyond the satirical jabs at existing religion and society, did not exist in the comix crowd. Far from it.

Thus Justin Green would devote vast art to his wanderings, from his own boyhood as a half-Jew to a deeply conflicted and mysterious connection to the Virgin Mary. Altogether connected with his teenage angst, religious confusion roiled his poor alter ego, Binky Brown. Crumb also wondered as he wandered. He disbelieved on principle, and yet expressed a cartoony vision of some ultimate truth, something ineffable that could almost be grasped . . . if never quite. It was the sentiment of a generation, and it influenced the quality of art as no previous generation of artists had self-consciously perceived it, almost as if *Little Nemo in Slumberland*, back in the visionary 1910s, had been part of an expansive genre and not sui generis.

what underground comix would become. Rivers was naturally despised and attacked by Clement Greenberg, guardian of an existing art world order soon to be overthrown by larger forces.

The introduction of everyday icons onto gallery walls, the critique of American culture and technological capitalism, was already in the air. Unlike their comic strip and comic book precursors (in general and with exceptions on both sides), the underground artists did mostly go to art school and presumably took in many of these influences, at some level. Most of them had to find their way back to comics.

Art Spiegelman, most prominently, was to say about his own early work that the great obstacle and then accomplishment was the need to become "cartoony," situated artistically in the world of the vernacular 1910s–40s. Crumb was already there instinctively, driven aeons farther into new territory by taking LSD while recapturing childhood memories of comics art. Aline Kominsky Crumb would speak for others when she reflected that her art-school lessons "didn't take." Most of the underground artists, it is fair to say, negotiated the distance between ends of the spectrum.

There is so much variation within the setting of the few comix titles available in 1968, to the dozen or so by early 1969 to the hundreds by 1972, that generalizations about the art can rightly be viewed with skepticism. What made Gilbert Shelton most unique, for instance, was his early, rare ability to tell a story. There was virtually nothing linear in the inspired drawings of Victor Moscoso or John Thompson. Most artists stood

The totality of a certain infernal art, the violence, homosexuality, and beyond-transgressive quality of S. Clay Wilson, the childlike horror of Rory Hayes, and the intensive corpse-mangling art of *Thrilling Murder*, among others, was new to comic art, though essentially an extension of the earlier pulps' lowest levels. Truly new, and painfully related, was *Slow Death*, a series that treated ecological exhaustion and its consequences, an ecological horror beyond any earlier human (or nonhuman) fate, with artists like Greg Irons driving home the point with didactic ferocity. Comics had always been "entertaining" by their nature, except perhaps when (as in issues of the Catholic *Treasure Chest* with martyrs boiled in oil) likely to be bought by parents for their children.

The women's liberation comic, beginning in 1970 with *It Ain't Me Babe*, found a successor in the series *Women's Liberation Comics* (and spin-off eroto-comic *Wet Satin*) and friendly competitor *Tits & Clits* (from Laguna Beach), which was immediately unique in its several approaches. The very idea of a cover with women in a demonstration around the White House, holding up their vibrators (*Tits & Clits* no. 3), was as stunning as sex had ever been in the raunchiest (male) underground comix. And the accomplishment was more than that.

Remembered painfully by some male and female contemporaries as narrowing or ideological—shunted aside from the mainstream, the women worked or acted as a counter-clique—it comprised a wide breadth, from the historical studies of Sharon Rudahl and Trina Robbins to the gross-out/fat-woman genre of Lee Marrs to the self-reflecting, I-was-a-teenager material of the two artists most personally uncomfortable in the feminist setting, Aline Kominsky Crumb and Diane Noomin (aka Newman). There was even the occasional rape fantasy. But what impressed more was the excavation of historic women's icons (Rosie the Riveter and Wonder Woman, for example) on the one hand, and the steady self-revelation about daily life on the other, usually with a dose of fantasy thrown in. Robbins's own considerable scholarship of women cartoonists would show, in later years, that a body of work had existed, although always scattered and discontinuous. There had never been such a concentrated, self-conscious role for women artists anywhere in the canon or outside it before 1970, and comix arguably offered as great an achievement as any of the rapidly advancing women's arts—except that its volume diminished so quickly, leaving most of the artists stranded.

Something special needs to be said about a single line of comics, *Dopin' Dan*, not only because it touched on the most blue-collar section of the antiwar movement, disaffected GIs themselves, but because Ted Richards did something so special with the *Beetle Bailey* tradition of comic strips, itself a far cry from *Steve Canyon* on the one hand, and Kurtzman's *Frontline Combat* on the other. Dopin' Dan the character, his buddies, his nemesis in the officer corps, and the role of dope in the whole story offered evidence that repression worked clumsily: These were definitely the most dangerous comics published.

Others intended to be altogether that political. *Conspiracy Capers*, edited in 1969 by the seemingly laugh-a-minute Skip

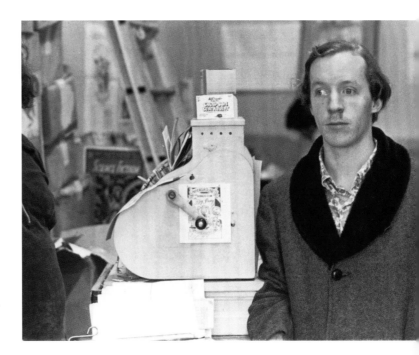

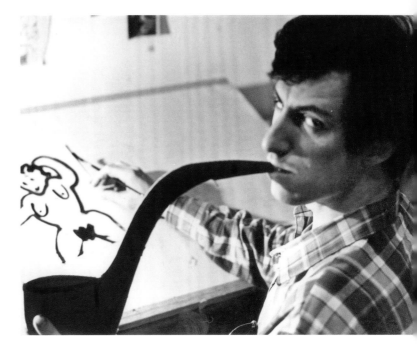

OPPOSITE | SKIP WILLIAMSON, 1976

TOP | RORY HAYES
at Gary Arlington's San Francisco Comic Book Company, 1973

BOTTOM | JUSTIN GREEN, 1972

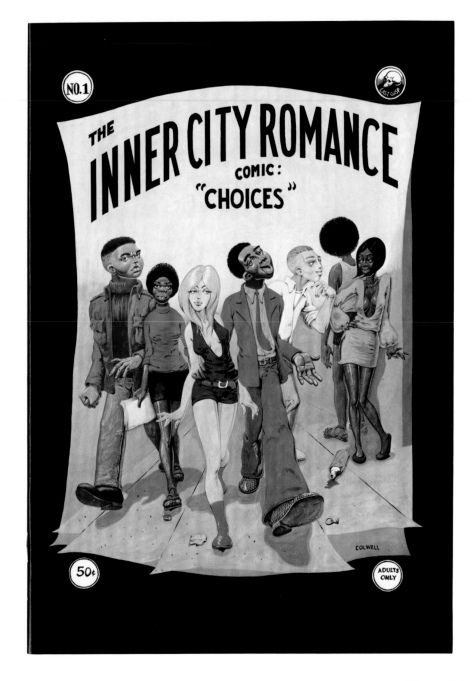

ABOVE | GUY COLWELL
The Inner City Romance Comic no. 1: "Choices," cover, 1972

OPPOSITE | ROBERT CRUMB
Arcade no. 2, cover, 1975

Williamson, had actually been published to raise money for the Chicago Eight, on trial for conspiracy. Artist Guy Colwell, in jail for draft resistance, created *Inner City Romance* as ghetto drama, although the politics tended to slip aside. Even *Radical America Komiks* had been aimed at achieving a political goal (and was shipped automatically to chapters of the Students for a Democratic Society), though sliding off into more familiar underground satire.

Not everything remarkable was so new or different. The close examination of details for the sake of precise satirical observations—nowhere better realized than in the work of Bill Griffith, with his Zippy alter ego—could be directly traced back to *MAD*, the genius of Kurtzman, Elder, Wallace Wood, and others returned with more freedom to explore sexuality and politics. Basics remained so familiar that the pages of *Young Lust*, coedited by Jay Kinney and Bill Griffith, could well have been *MAD* redux, ruthlessly revisited with lightening effects of *MAD* swept away and the radical core of the original recaptured. By the time Art Spiegelman's "Ace Hole, Midget Detective" appeared in Denis Kitchen's short-lived *Comix Book*, the ability to merge *MAD*-style scrutiny with Postmodern art had taken hold. The Air Pirates crowd, a group of cartoonists founded by Dan O'Neill and responsible for the litigious *Air Pirates Funnies*, did not so much satirize Mickey Mouse and other Disney characters as add something to them, something seen to be missing.

To me, *American Splendor* is the most enduring underground offering, both in its recuperation and its transformation of the original comic form. Harvey Pekar, who began his widely heralded series in 1976, near the end of the underground comics movement proper, was in a way the ultimate in self-description. Unlike Spain Rodriguez, who could write powerfully about blue-collar/delinquent life in 1950s Buffalo but also in a range of different genres, Pekar had only himself as subject (and he did not draw). He had been there in a different sense from the beginning, of course, as an intimate of R. Crumb. With the 2003 film *American Splendor*, a certain memory of the underground was recuperated as perhaps nowhere else that is ever likely to be on the big screen. Too bad, in some sense, that it was a memory of Cleveland, worlds away from the main scene of action in San Francisco, about which we still have few histories and no novels, graphic or otherwise. But we do have seven issues of *Arcade*, which ran from 1975 to 1977, whose contents may be said to have best summed up what the underground had been and what it left behind.

The cultural deflation of the early 1970s, as well as the associated degree of political repression, can scarcely be understood by those who came after. It seemed to many observers (myself included) that the best poetry, music, and art all hit a brick wall and bounced back. The huge tragedy was that the undergrounds had been cut off in the most promising moment of development, as surely as the *Masses* artists had faced jail and literary suppression. That earlier handful of rebellious artists mostly found their way, professionally, albeit with a social movement. The large majority of underground artists stopped drawing, or at least stopped publishing, only a decade after their emergence. Kitchen Sink Press, Last Gasp, and Rip Off Press struggled to keep things going and found assorted means, including anthologies and merchandise, to fit a number of the underground artists in the comics collector or comics fan circuit, bridging the gap to the 1990s generation of young artists and beyond. The losses, nevertheless, were staggering.

Arcade partners Griffith and Spiegelman have come to symbolize so much between them in the subsequent history of comics art that it may be forgotten how wide the sweep of *Arcade* extended or what its deepest purposes (not always conscious) may have been. Certainly it was the life raft thrown out to the sinking underground art world, as the two intended. But it was a great deal more, as well.

One of the keenest moments in Crumb's early burst of glory was a comic that reminded readers, on the back cover, that comics are "only lines on paper." Never overwhelmingly modest—but definitely given to moments of self-denigration and even contempt—Crumb was not so much satirizing as explaining. Comics, in early form, were a product of the collective genius that the individual artist drew into himself or herself. Some potential artists naturally had more talent than others, but the low reputation of the comic-art form possessed a great positive side as well. Comics artists never really got far from their working class origins, not even if they wanted to, not even (as an older Crumb might have observed) when a drawing on a restaurant placemat is worth thousands of dollars.

Thus, *Arcade* can be seen as an instruction booklet in a language that had never been recognized—certainly, not in the United States—as a language. Almost from beginning to end, along with making a little money for the artists of a fast-fading genre, it was meant to instruct. Or, perhaps, its editors and many of its artists could not help trying to do so, increasingly aware that this was the last big chance to make the necessary points. Every issue included an old-time reprint—the most attention such features had been given since the days of *Help!*—from *Little Nemo* to the Tijuana Bibles. Most every issue included some cracked classic, a satire on the *Classics Illustrated* series that was two or three times more satirical by playing upon other genres.

One of the great tragedies of *Arcade*'s demise is that its end-of-the-book section, so much like a similar section of *Help!*, was once more an artistic incubator, this time often for women artists in particular. But *Arcade* was the end of the line for a generation, even if newer experiments (such as the educational *All-Atomic Comic* series, launched in 1976, leading to Leonard Rifas's *Educomics*) emerged just as *Arcade* went into its death throes. Among those following closely were the wonderfully inventive *Anarchy*

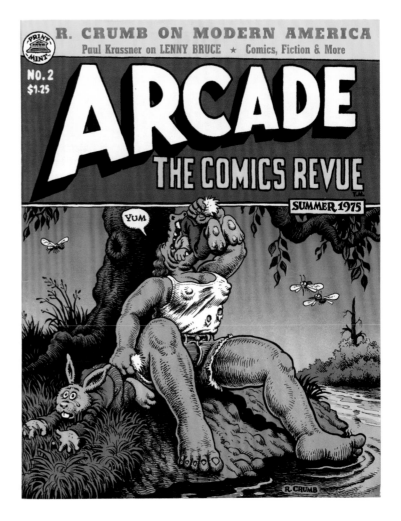

Comics (from 1978, edited by Jay Kinney and Paul Mavrides), *Gay Comix* (1980, the work of Howard Cruse, later to be known for the signal gay/civil rights novel, *Stuck Rubber Baby*), Larry Gonick's *Cartoon History of the Universe* (first volume published in 1978), *World War 3 Illustrated* (first published in 1979), and of course, *RAW* magazine and *Maus* (both launched in 1980).

At best, publisher/distributors like Kitchen Sink reached their specialized audience through an occasional bookstore presence and mailing lists that foreshadowed the rise of Fantagraphics. At worst, they were the artistic outpourings of a lost generation, able to achieve only a portion of what the comix revolution of 1969 had promised and would have delivered, in other circumstances, on talent alone. There were so many larger losses in these years—the receding waves of social transformation, the transfer of "sexual freedom" into license, the vogue of LSD into cocaine, the reconsolidation of corporate prestige in Ronald Reagan and the restart of the Cold War—that a tragedy in the vernacular art world (or any art world) cannot be taken too seriously. But for those of us who miraculously relived the most pleasureful moments of childhood, watching for new items to appear, poring over them with enthusiasm and an adult awareness that the vernacular was reaching up toward a reconciliation of the artists' hand and the intellectuals' vision, it was a blow not to be underestimated. Just now—beyond midlife, thirty years on, with the Web at full cruising speed and the promise of a new graphic novel art on the horizon—we may be recovering. ∎

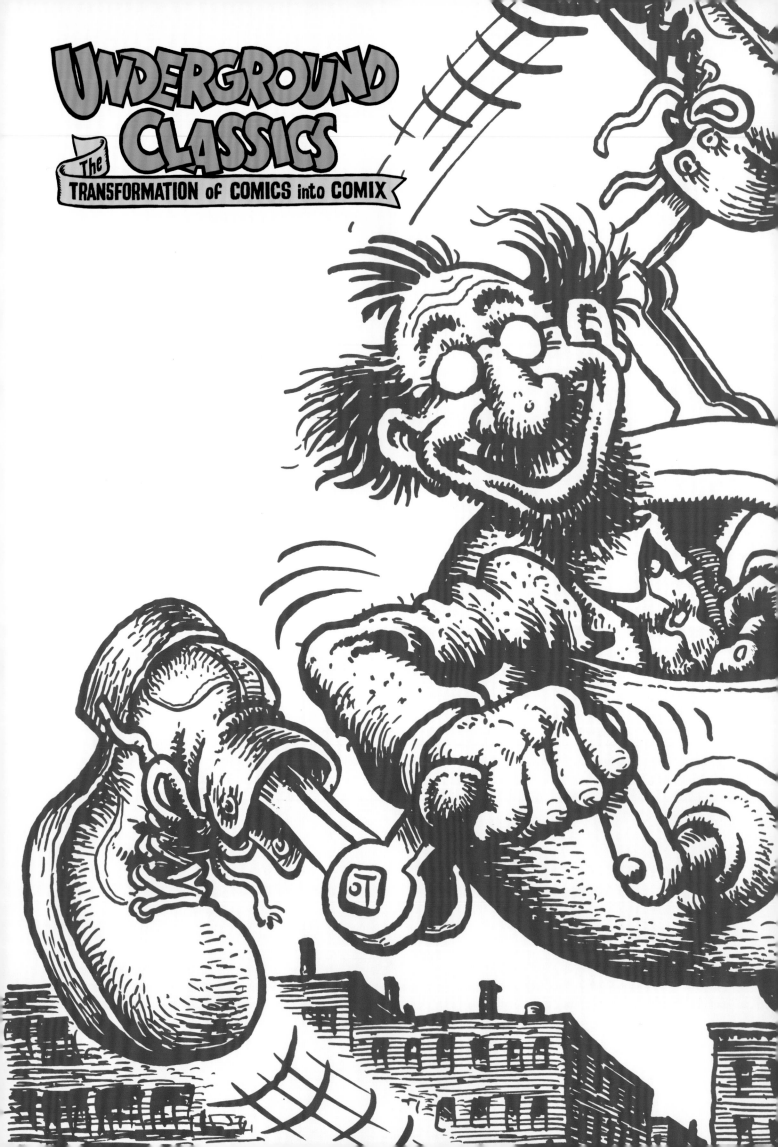

UNDERGROUND CLASSICS

The

TRANSFORMATION of COMICS into COMIX

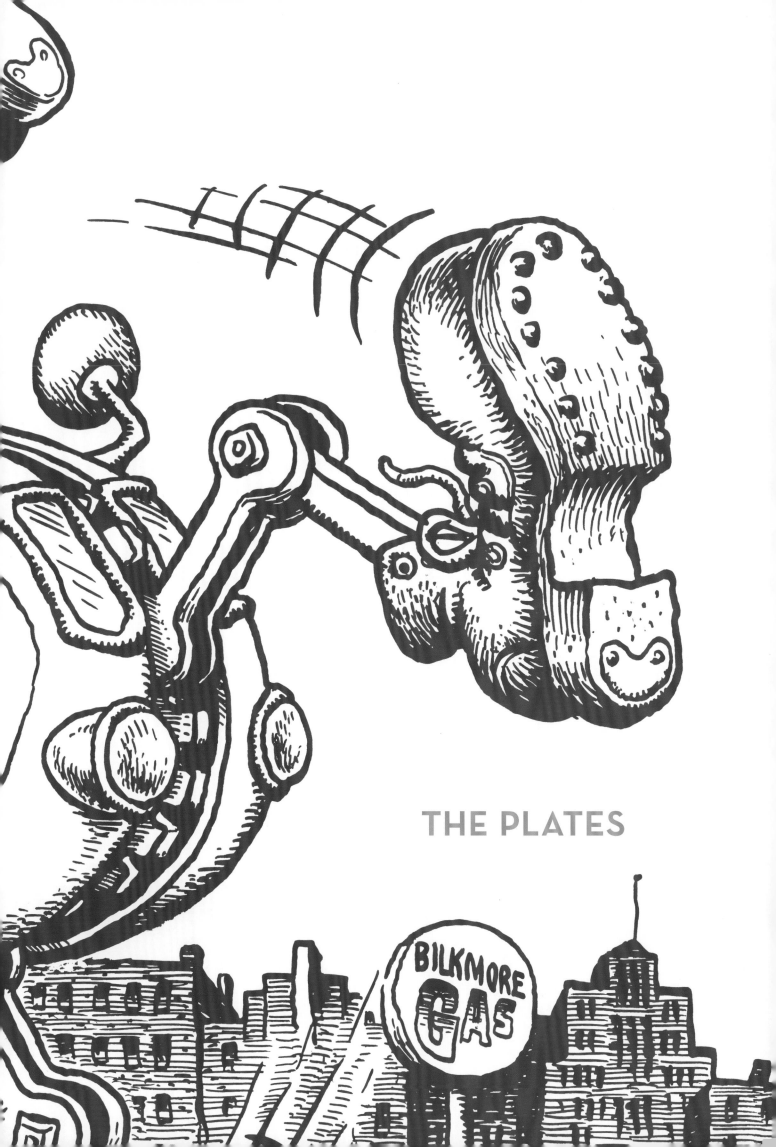

THE PLATES

BILKMORE GAS

JOEL BECK

"The Rise and Fall and Rise and Fall and Rise and Fall of the American Revolution," 1972; Opposite: "One Dong's Family," 1976

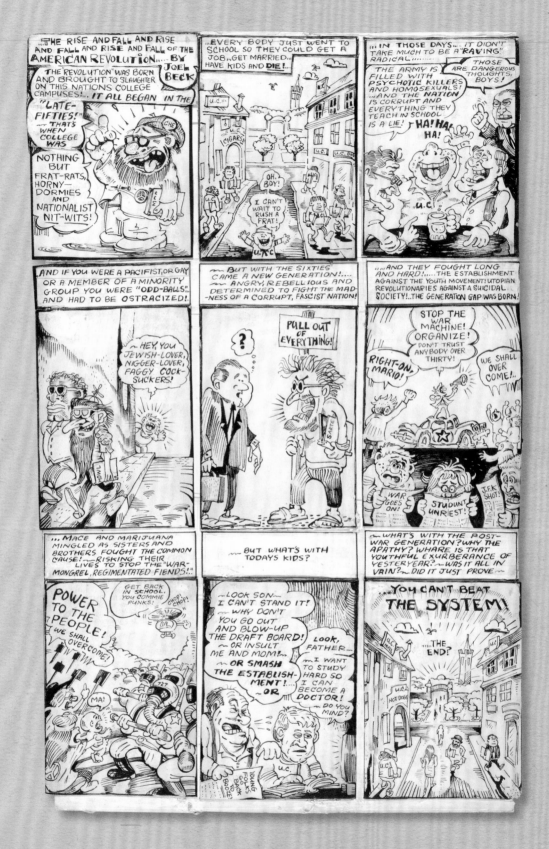

Pen and ink | 10 × 16 inches

Foreshadowing the politics of the sixties were the 1964–65 student protests on the University of California, Berkeley campus, inspired by the Freedom Riders who traveled to the South to help African Americans fight for their civil rights. Joel Beck, who was on the scene, later offered this observation of Mario Savio's Free Speech Movement and the tendency toward conformity and apathy.

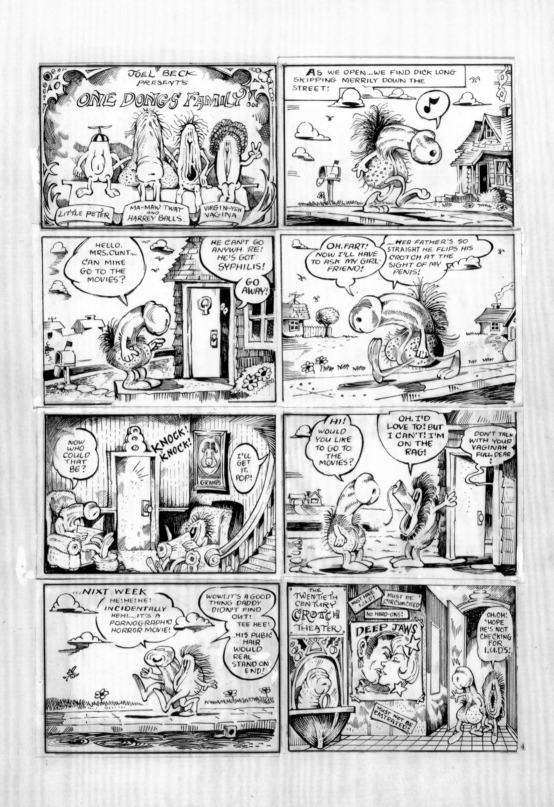

Pen and ink | 13 × 18 ½ inches

Turning conventional *Ozzie and Harriet* or *Leave It to Beaver* visions of the All-American family on its head, Beck offers an outrageous parody wherein the All-American unit is presented as a family of genitals. The short story appeared in the popular anthology *Bizarre Sex*.

Joel Beck, Richard Corben, Kim Deitch, Aline Kominsky Crumb, Trina Robbins, Gilbert Shelton

Famous Cartoonist Button Series, 1974

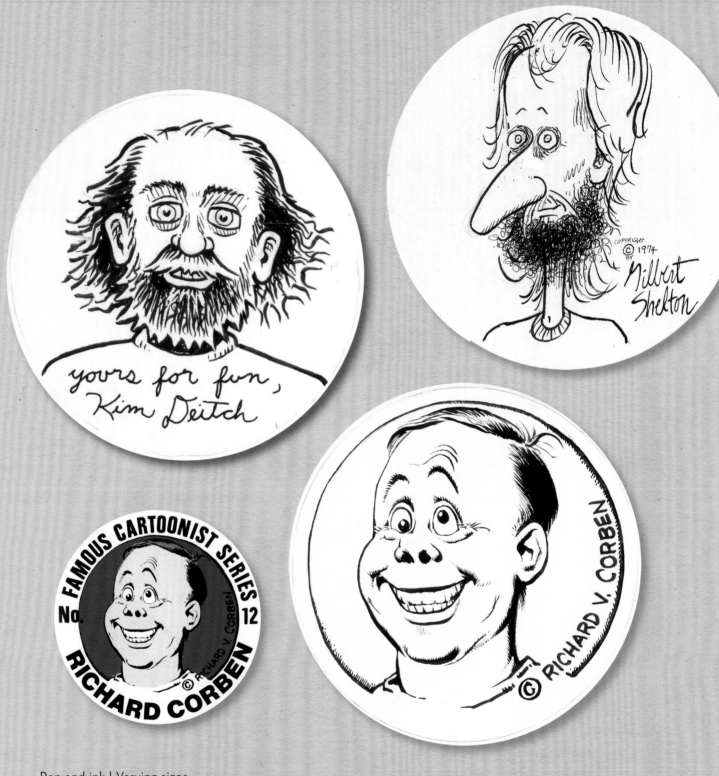

yours for fun,
Kim Deitch

COPYRIGHT
© 1974
BY
Gilbert
Shelton

FAMOUS CARTOONIST SERIES
NO. 12
RICHARD CORBEN
© RICHARD V. CORBEN

© RICHARD V. CORBEN

Pen and ink | Varying sizes

These drawings were among the fifty-four in Kitchen Sink Press's "Famous Cartoonist Button Series," laboriously manufactured using a manual punch press. Cartoonists, unlike their fine-art counterparts, seldom take themselves too seriously, particularly when drawing themselves. Take, for instance, Richard Corben's less-than-flattering self-portrait. Gilbert Shelton could easily be mistaken for the fourth Freak Brother, and Kim Deitch's straightforward self-portrait is that of an archetypal hippie of the period. Joel Beck, with a wink, strikes a jaunty pose with a straw hat and cigarette holder. Aline Kominsky Crumb chooses to depict herself with a sneer, while Trina Robbins's self-portrait resembles a bespectacled Sheena, Queen of the Jungle, with a clenched, dripping brush substituted for a dagger.

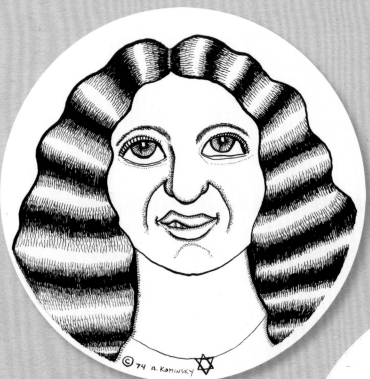

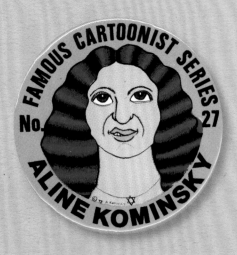

FAMOUS CARTOONIST SERIES
No. 27
ALINE KOMINSKY

© '74 A. KOMINSKY

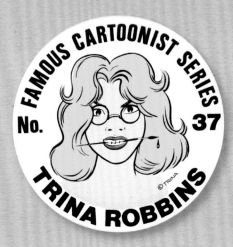

FAMOUS CARTOONIST SERIES
No. 37
TRINA ROBBINS

© TRINA

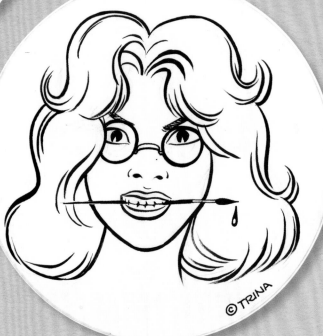

© TRINA

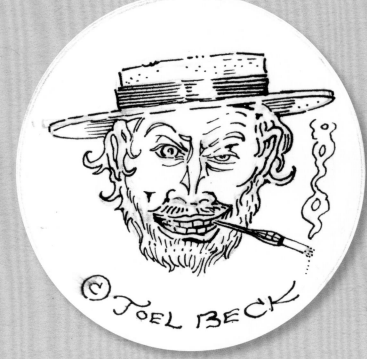

© JOEL BECK

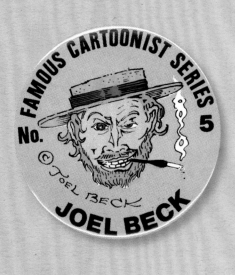

FAMOUS CARTOONIST SERIES
No. 5
JOEL BECK

VAUGHN BODE

"Love Is Thee," 1971; Opposite: "Cheech Wizard: Da' Terminal Trick," 1975

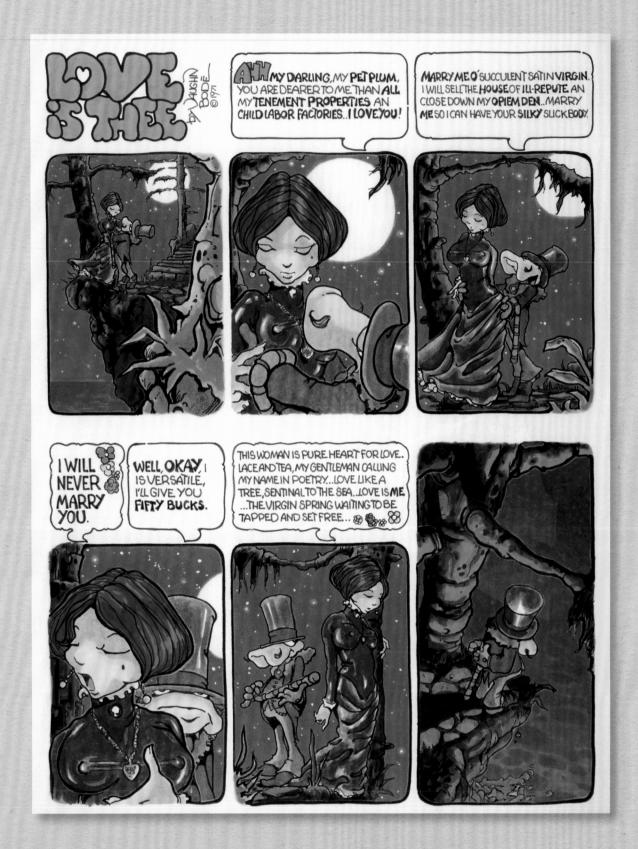

Color markers | 14 × 19 inches

This page from *Deadbone Erotica* no doubt annoyed some comix readers in the growing women's liberation movement, but in a battle of wills between a scummy male suitor and a high-and-mighty woman, the winner, to the cartoonist, is dark humor. Vaughn Bode effectively allows the viewer to imagine what happens between the final panels.

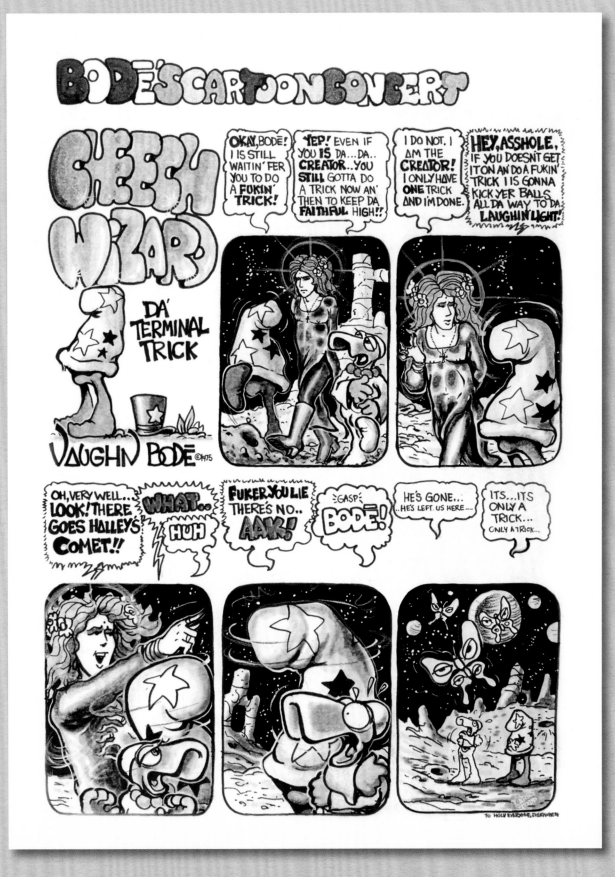

Black and gray markers | 9½ × 14¼ inches

In the 1970s, *National Lampoon* magazine, which originated as an outgrowth of the *Harvard Lampoon*, brought a new style of parody to American readers and made space for new kinds of comic strips, such as *Cheech Wizard*, about a lizard whose body is overwhelmed by a large hat. Cheech became Vaughn Bodé's most iconic creation. In this page the artist inserts himself in the strip but pulls "the terminal trick" and disappears from the comics page. In a final irony, Bodé died the year he created this page.

TIM BOXELL

Commies From Mars: The Red Planet! no. 1, cover, 1972

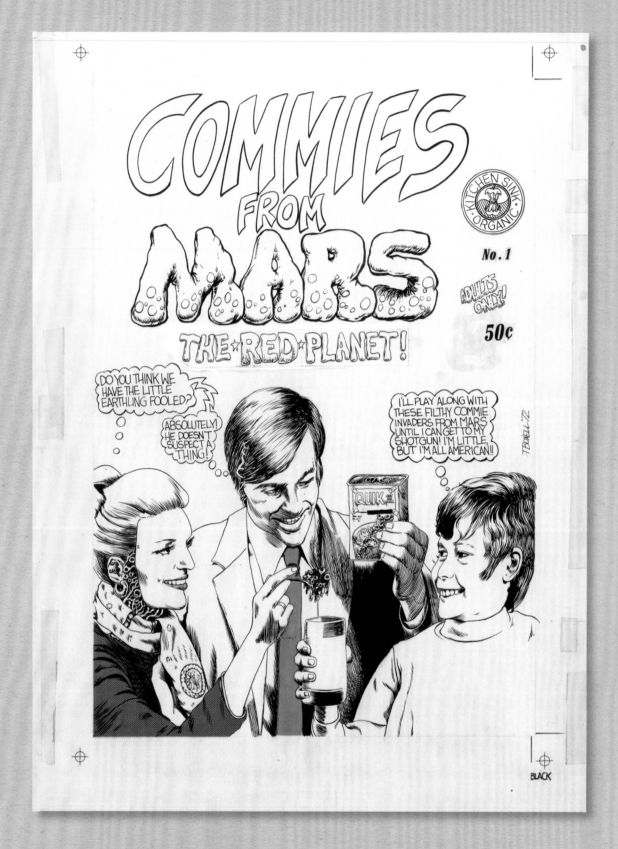

Pen and ink with Zip-A-Tone | 11 × 15 inches

Tim Boxell, a Minneapolis-based comix artist, writer, and editor whose art was sometimes signed "Grisly," is perhaps best known for his underground comix adaptation of the novel *The Image of the Beast*. He was the editor as well as contributor to *Commies From Mars*. In this debut cover, Boxell parodies a combination of McCarthyite and space-invasion fears. Boxell went on to become a movie director and designer. His credits include *Brenda Starr* (1989) and *Chasing Destiny* (2001).

Banzai! no. 1, cover, 1978

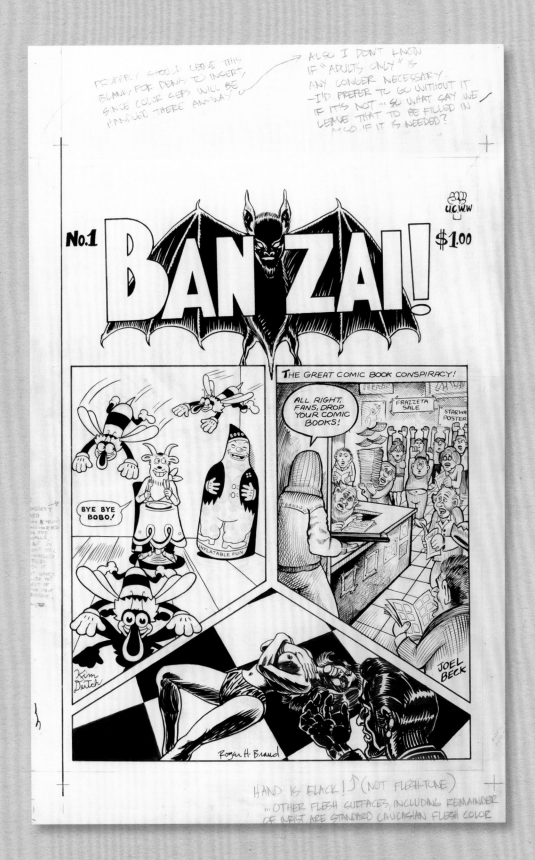

Brush, pen, and ink | 14½ × 23 inches

Making ironic use here of the best-known war cry of Japanese soldiers during World War II, many underground cartoonists ferociously attacked mainstream American culture. This unusual cover is a rare example of a cartoon triptych. The picture pane is divided three ways, with each artist—Roger Brand, Joel Beck, and Kim Deitch—doing a solo drawing. This is distinct from interactive "jams," in which multiple artists draw over, under, or around one another's work within the same page or panel.

CHARLES BURNS

Dope Comix no. 5, cover, 1982

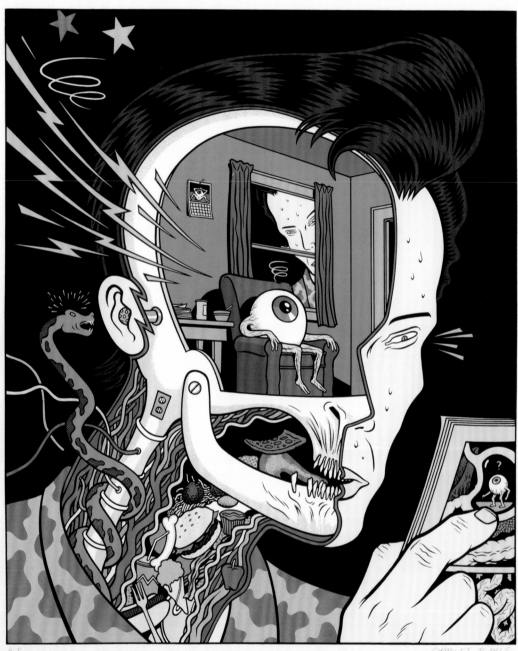

Serigraph, signed | 24 × 27 inches

In this silk-screen version of Charles Burns's introspective cover, the viewer is taken inside the head of someone who has likely consumed the mind-altering substances that were popular at the time and that helped define the underground subculture. But all things come to an end; this illustration marked the last issue of *Dope Comix*. By the early eighties the head shops that sold rolling papers, pipes, and other accoutrements for smoking marijuana were rapidly closing down because of increasingly restrictive ordinances as well as a changing culture.

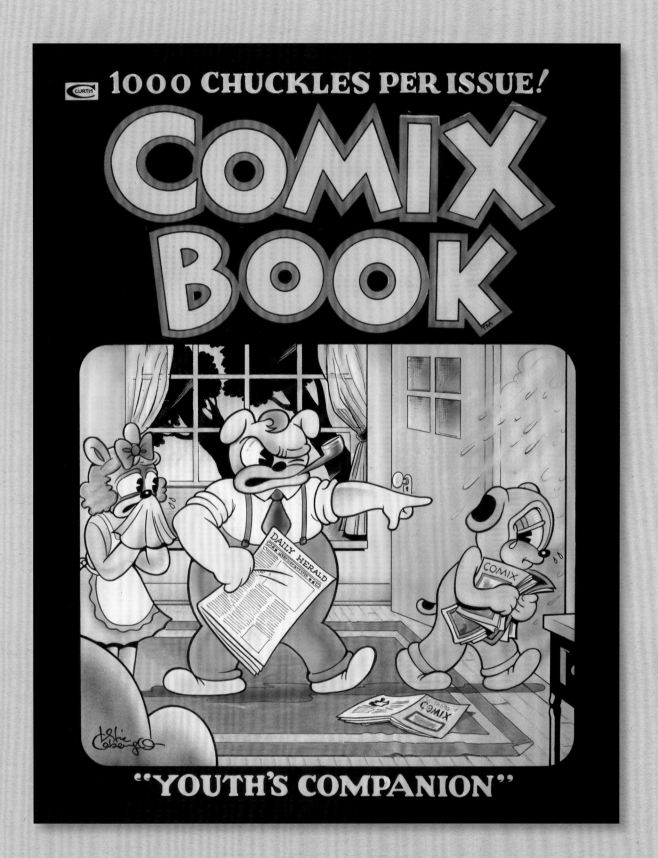

Brush and ink with airbrushed color | 14¾ × 19 inches

In 1973 Stan Lee, longtime editor in chief at Marvel Comics and legendary co-creator of Spider-Man and the Fantastic Four, invited Denis Kitchen to create a "hybrid" title for his line—one that would tap into the energy of the undergrounds while not sullying Marvel's family-friendly reputation. *Comix Book* was the experimental result. This is the cover for the fourth of five issues. Leslie Cabarga depicts a tragic scene all too familiar to many young comic book fans: a comic book collector in conflict with his disapproving parents.

Leslie Cabarga

Dope Comix no. 1, cover, 1978

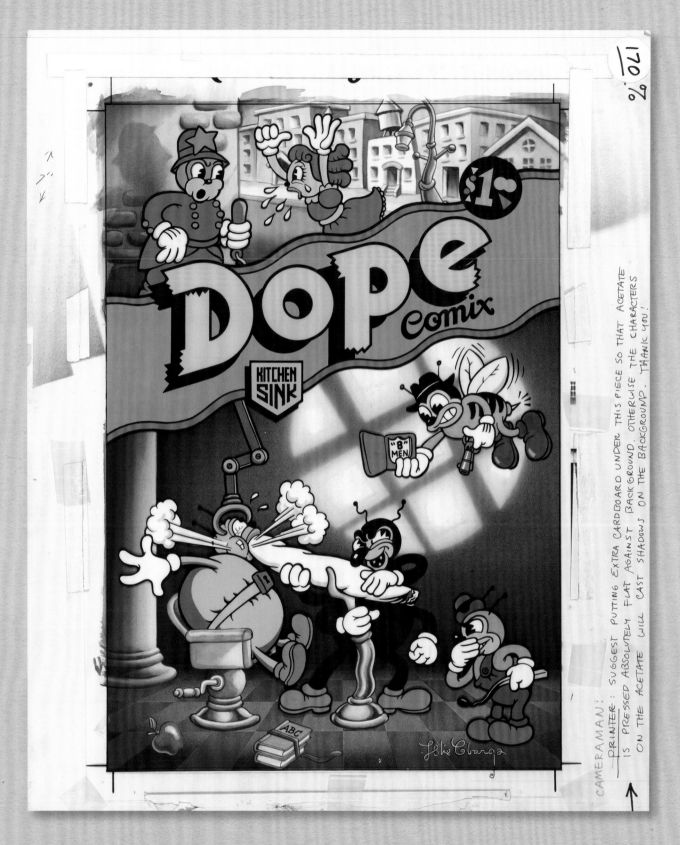

Line art on acetate over airbrushed background | 14 × 17 ¾ inches

Tapping into the pervasive drug culture and wide popularity of magazines like *High Times* and *Head*, Kitchen Sink Press produced the unabashed *Dope Comix* series, which found a ready audience in head shops across America and beyond. Leslie Cabarga here parodies drug dealers and paranoia while utilizing the 1930s cartoon style of the Max Fleischer animation studio. This cover was also issued as a poster, which adorned many dorm and apartment walls.

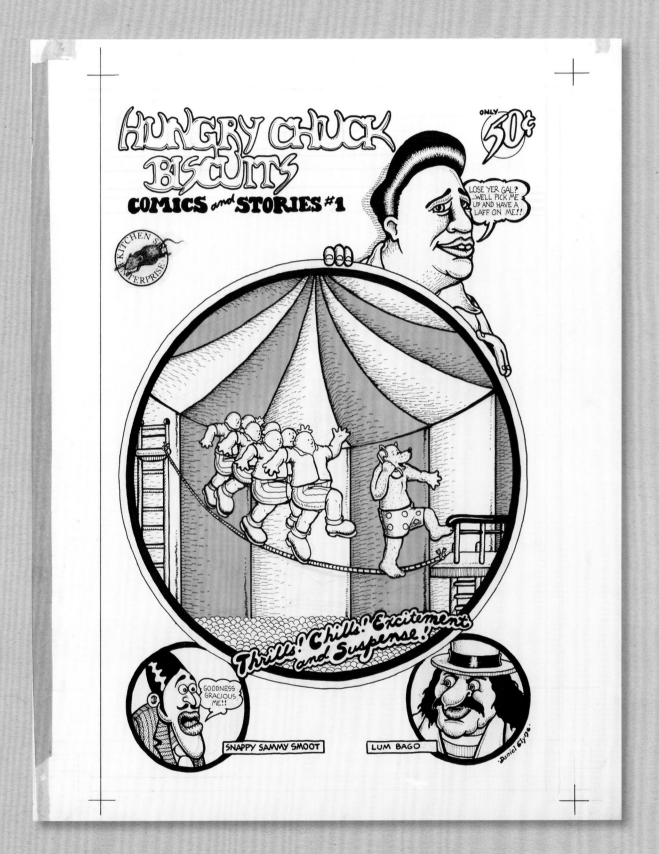

Pen and ink with Zip-A-Tone | 12 × 15½ inches

The short-lived Kumquat Productions imprint floundered when its prospective investor read the "Hungry Chuck Biscuits" contribution to *Shangri-La* no. 1, in which Chuck, a generally gross teenager, graphically expels intestinal worms. Dan Clyne's solo title for his signature character was eventually, and successfully, published by Kitchen Sink Press. This unpublished cover art was drawn primarily by Clyne, but Skip Williamson provided a cameo of his own signature character, Snappy Sammy Smoot, as a guest feature.

RICHARD CORBEN

"To Meet the Faces You Meet," 1972

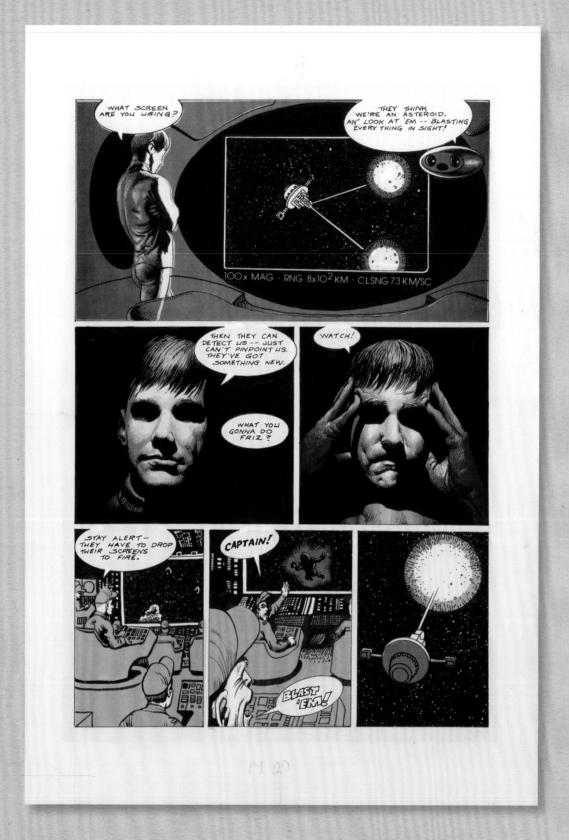

Brush and ink with Zip-A-Tone | 12 × 15½ inches

This page from the cover story of *Fever Dreams* no. 1, written by Jan Strnad, concerns a beetle-like spaceship and its strange inhabitants, Frierson and Meade. Frierson is a deformed cripple, but the robot, Meade, projects an illusory reality in which he appears as a handsome lover surrounded by beautiful women. Richard Corben, the most well-known exemplar of science-fiction undergrounds, has appeared frequently in *Heavy Metal* and many European publications, making him an international figure.

Robert Crumb

Self-portrait, 1969

SHEEIT!
R. CRUMB
SELF PORTRAIT
'69

Pen and ink | 16 × 19 inches

In this early self-portrait, R. Crumb sums up his attitude of the moment with a simple "Sheeit!" Though stand-alone self-portraits like this are uncommon, Crumb has included himself extensively in his stories. Artists throughout history have put themselves in their work, but comix tend to particularly lend themselves to this mode of self-expression, where the artist can be part of the frame both visually and through his words. Crumb has chronicled his experiences and fantasies to the extent that his life is a virtual open book to his readers.

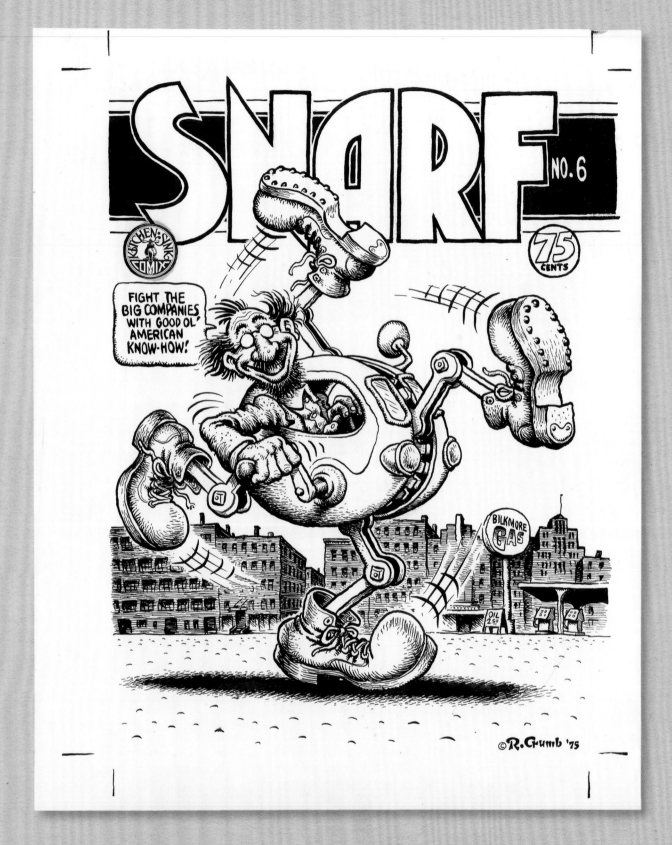

Pen and ink | 23¼ × 29¼ inches

R. Crumb's version of a mad (but not evil) cartoon scientist answers the mid-seventies version of the energy crisis and spiraling gas prices with a simple solution: the most compact of motor vehicles. Both the subject and the satire remain as topical today as three decades ago.

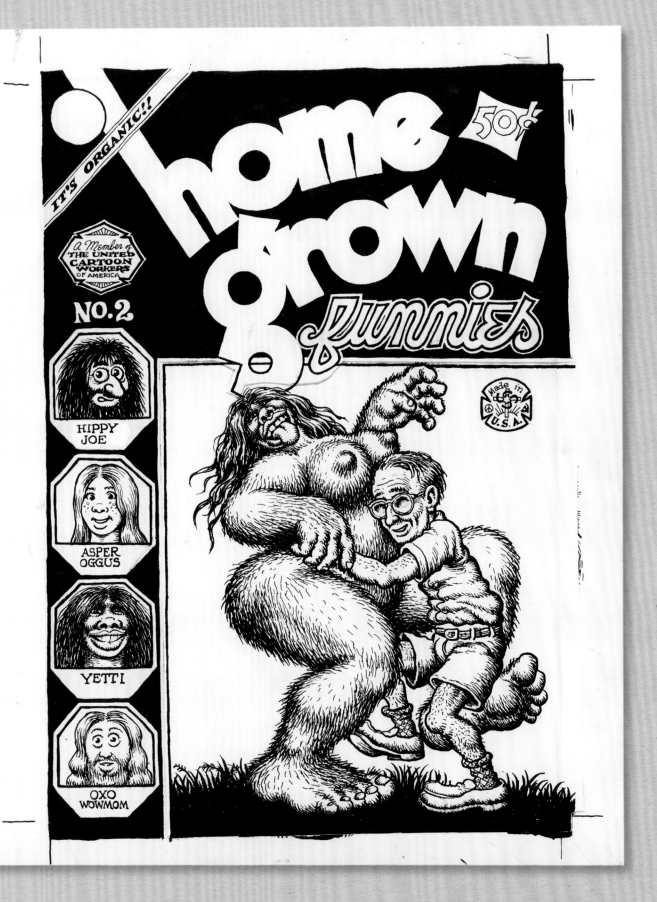

Pen and ink | 11 × 14 inches

The artist's self-portrait with Yetti is from an unpublished cover. Many of Crumb's comix include dominant women, an admitted fetish, such as Angelfood McSpade, a gigantic black female with an unbridled sexual appetite; the satanic Devil Girl; and here, Yetti, a passionate Bigfoot introduced in the "Whiteman" episode of *Home Grown Funnies* no. 1. This intended sequel was never finished. An authorized screenplay based on Yetti and Whiteman was written but likewise never developed.

HOWARD CRUSE

"Wendel: March on Washington," 1988; Opposite: "Wendel: The Fagbasher," 1989

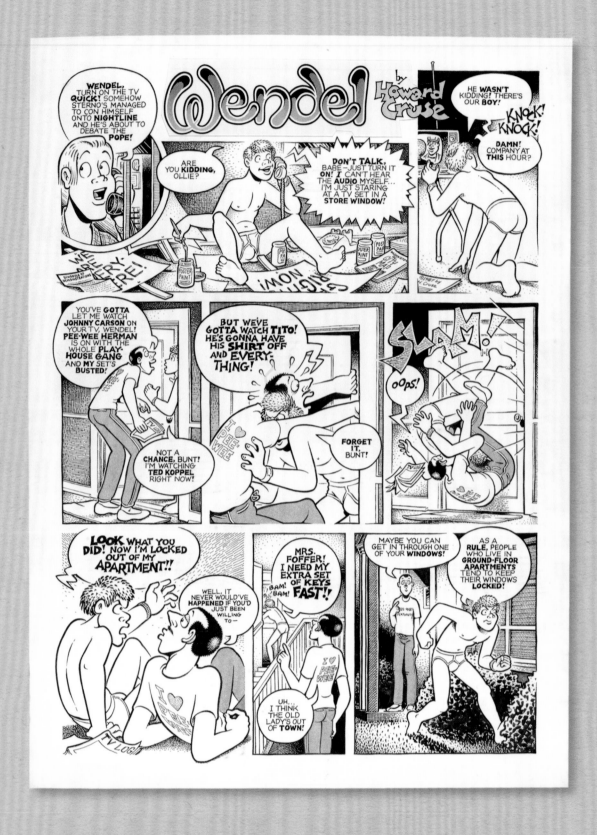

Pen and ink with Zip-A-Tone | each 14½ × 20 inches

Howard Cruse, the foremost gay underground cartoonist, is perhaps best known for his acclaimed graphic novel *Stuck Rubber Baby* (Paradox Press, 1995), centering on growing up gay in Alabama during the civil rights movement. His early artist character Headrack "came out" in *Barefootz Funnies* no. 2 (1976), long before popular culture included gay people to any significant degree. Cruse went on to edit and contribute to *Gay Comix* (1980), the first such anthology. His later *Wendel* pages are arguably his most accessible and popular works: Wendel and the primary cast are gay, but the strips have a universal human appeal.

Wendel
OH, SHIT!
THE FLEEING FAGBASHER HAS FAILED TO RECKON WITH THE FORCE OF A FLYING FAGOLA!
OW!
WHUMP!
©1989 by H. Cruse
WE'VE GOT 'IM PINNED!
ARE THE COPS COMIN'?
IS STERNO HURT?
HE'S SURE GOTTEN THE WIND KNOCKED OUT OF 'IM!
Gasp.. Pant..
LOST IN A NOT-WHOLLY-UNPLEASANT STUPOR GENERATED BY OXYGEN DEPRIVATION, STERNO IS SURPRISED TO HEAR A VOICE FROM THE DISTANT PAST...
THAT WAS QUITE A TACKLE YOU LAID ON THAT RASCAL, FELLA!
BOOSTER HIGH
WHY, IT'S THE GHOST OF OL' COACH DUDDY FROM BOOSTER HIGH —DEAD LO THESE MANY YEARS...
I TAKE BACK EVERYTHING I USED TO SAY ABOUT YOU! YOU'RE A REAL MAN!!
GEE, THANKS, COACH!
I GUESS THAT'S WHAT SUCKIN' A LITTLE DICK'LL DO FOR YA!
pat, pat!
BOOSTER HIGH
WE DON'T NEED ANOTHER AMBULANCE, DO WE?
HE'S SMILING! I GUESS THAT'S A GOOD SIGN...

KIM DEITCH

"Be-In" cover for the *East Village Other*, October 11, 1968

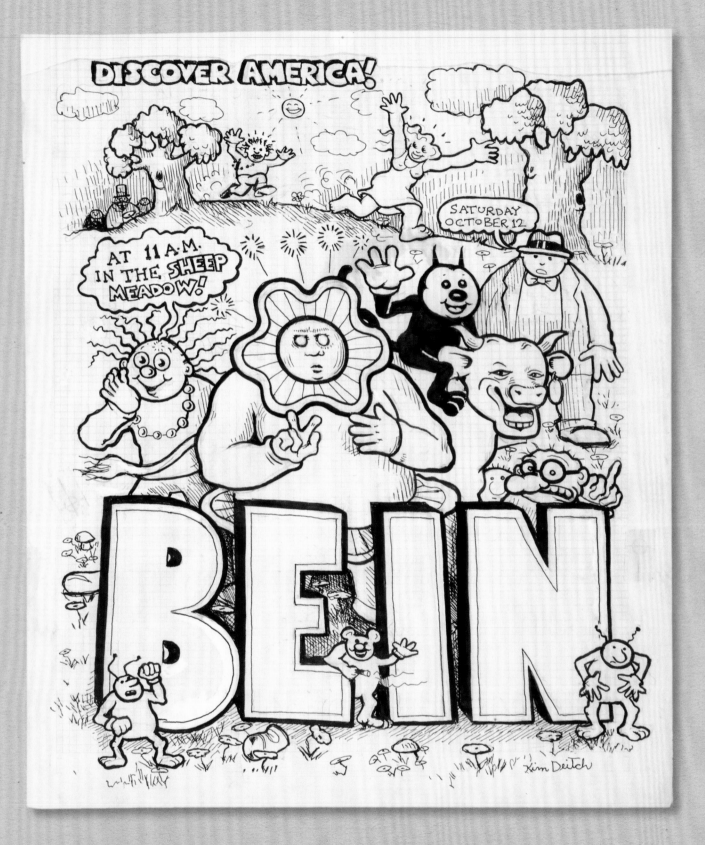

Pen and ink | 12 × 14 inches

San Francisco's Human Be-In of January 1967 was a historic development in American counterculture. On that day hippies and all manner of young and old gathered in Golden Gate Park to celebrate human empowerment, communal living, and higher consciousness (often achieved with chemical enhancements). Here Kim Deitch depicts a version of the Be-In in Central Park for New York's *East Village Other*. One of the original underground tabloids, *EVO* began publishing in 1965. These venues provided cartoonists with exposure prior to the late-sixties outburst of underground comix.

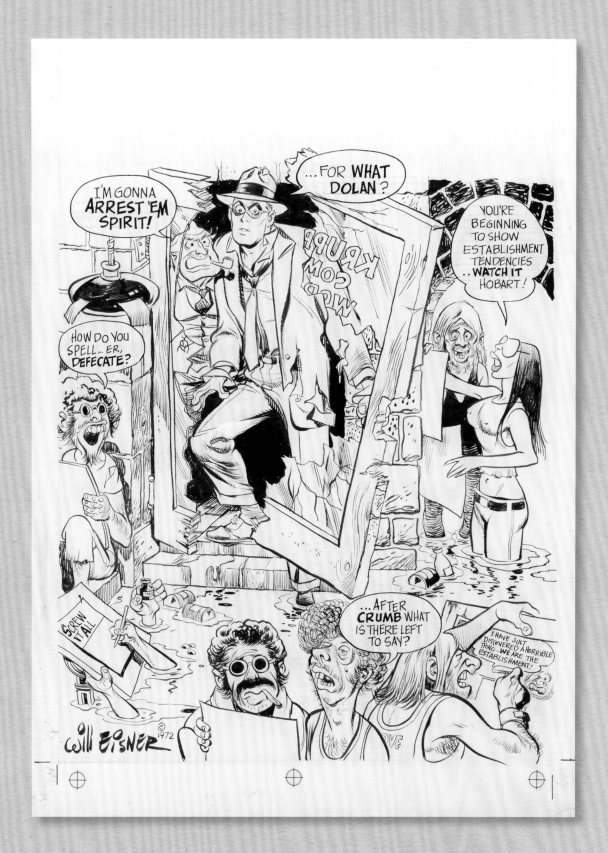

Brush and ink | 9 × 13 inches

Spirit creator Will Eisner, who influenced countless cartoonists, was himself influenced in mid-career by a movement of much younger artists. Inspired especially by the autobiographical undergrounds, Eisner jump-started the graphic novel phenomenon in 1978 with his *A Contract with God and Other Tenement Stories*. Here, Eisner's tongue-in-cheek cover has the Spirit and Police Commissioner Dolan breaking into the Kitchen Sink (Krupp Comic Works) office, located in an "underground" sewer.

WILL ELDER

Snarf no. 10, cover, 1987

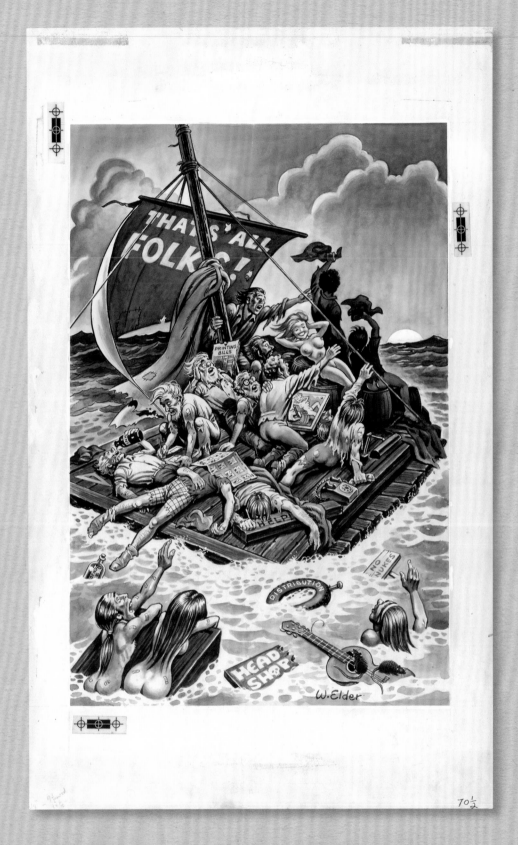

Ink, wash, and white watercolor | 12½ × 20 inches

Will Elder was an integral part of the legendary E.C. and *MAD* comics crew in the early 1950s and a longtime collaborator of Harvey Kurtzman, both of whom were venerated by underground cartoonists. Though not part of either the generation or the movement, Elder agreed to do this cover for the underground anthology *Snarf*. Parodying his favorite masterpiece, Théodore Gericault's *Raft of the Medusa*, Elder portrays a counterculture dying and adrift in the late eighties.

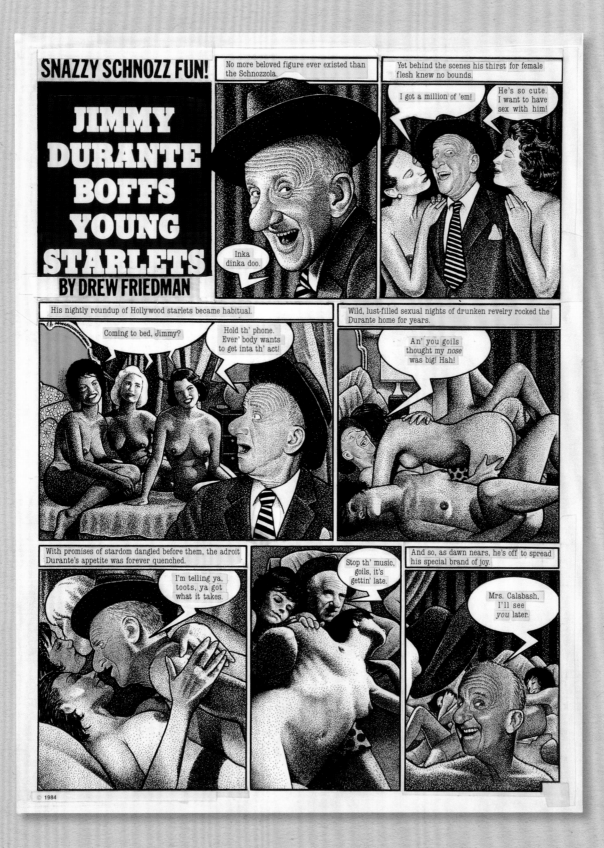

Pen and ink | 8 × 11 inches

Drew Friedman, a latecomer to the underground comix scene due to his younger age, is best known for his pointillist or "stippling" style of caricature, employing thousands of pen-marks to simulate the look of a photograph (although in recent years he has switched to a painted technique). His work has appeared widely, from *Blab!* to *Entertainment Weekly* to *MAD*. Friedman's painstaking attention to detail and photorealistic, incongruous parodies of Hollywood legends is sui generis. He was a student of both Harvey Kurtzman and Will Eisner at the School of Visual Arts.

Don Glassford, Robert Crumb, Jay Kinney, Denis Kitchen, Jay Lynch, Jim Mitchell, Bruce Walthers, Skip Williamson

"Let's Be Realistic Comics" jam, April 15, 1971

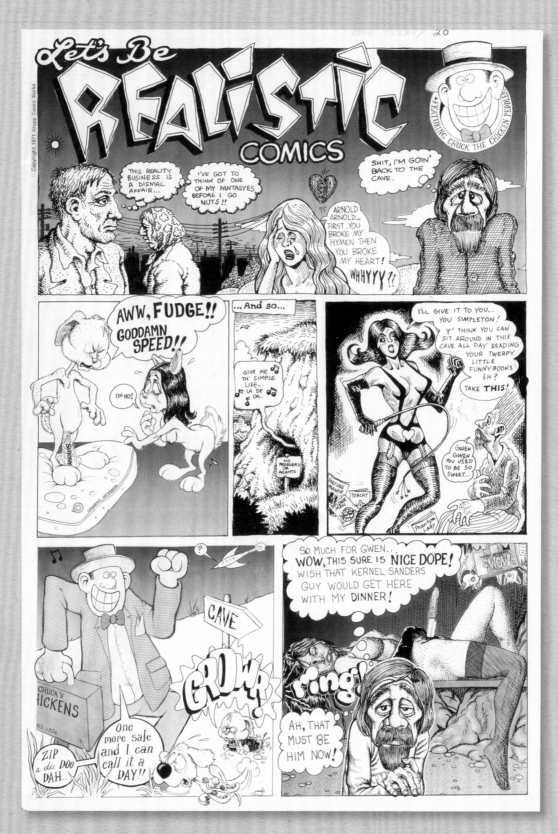

Brush, pen, and ink with Zip-A-Tone | 13 × 19¼ and 11 ½ × 17 inches

This two-page story is an example of spontaneous "jam" cartooning (loosely based on the improvisational jazz term), in which alternating panels and details are created by various artists, generally without serious regard to linear story or plot. Jams are typically, though not necessarily, created by artists working simultaneously while passing the art around a room, as in the case of this afternoon improvisation.

21
PAGE 21
SCHLOMP SCHLUMP SCHLUP!
WHAT'S THE USE?
I THOUGHT THIS WAS A REALISTIC COMIC...
SOLID
YEAH? WELL, HERE'S A LITTLE TASTE OF "REALITY" FOR YUH, YUH ALIEN CREEPO! HAW HAW!!
SPLAT
TSK TSK! WHY IS IT THAT YOU EARTHMEN ALWAYS RESORT TO VIOLENCE AT THE DROP OF A HAT? WHY IS IT? HUH?
YOU WASN'T WEARIN' NO HAT... BESIDES, IT'S JUST OUR WAY... ALLUS HAS BEEN... ALLUS WILL BE... YOU DON'T LIKE IT? GO BACK WHERE YUH CAME FROM!!
'N' I C'N EAT MORE CHICKEN 'N YEW EVER SEEN..
SEZ WHO?
SEZ ME!
I WANT TH' NECK AN' MY COUSIN ERNIE WANTS TH' WING AN' MY OL' LADY'S BROTHER WANTS TH' TAIL BONE AN...
I'm getting out of this crazy place with th' bill of goods before it's too late!
ZIT!
End

GRASS GREEN

"Wild Man Meets Rubberoy," 1971

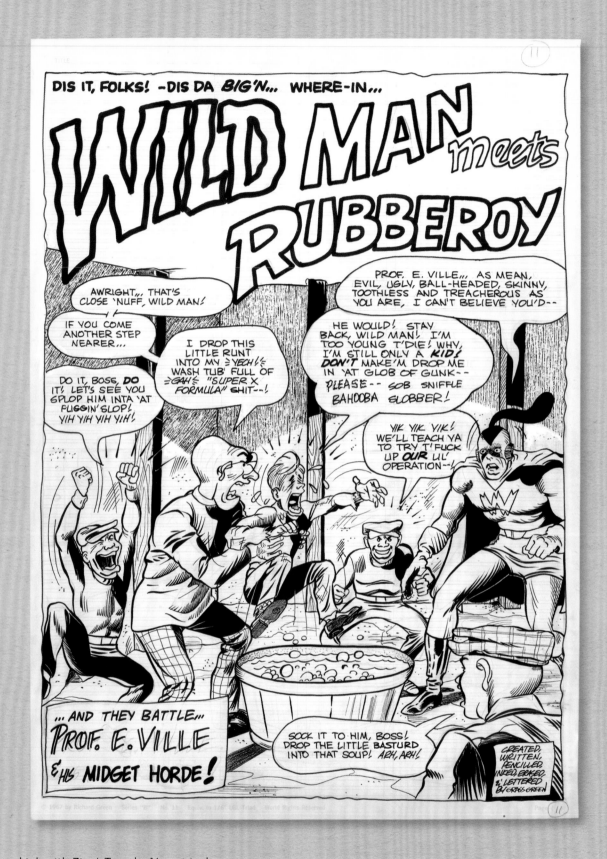

Pen and ink with Zip-A-Tone | 11½ × 16 inches

Richard "Grass" Green was an African-American and Midwestern (Indiana) underground cartoonist who created *Super-Soul Comix*, an idiosyncratic and risqué look at race in America. His characters Wild Man and Rubberoy grew out of Green's early involvement in comics' small but vital fanzine movement, which led to the first critical examinations of the comics medium.

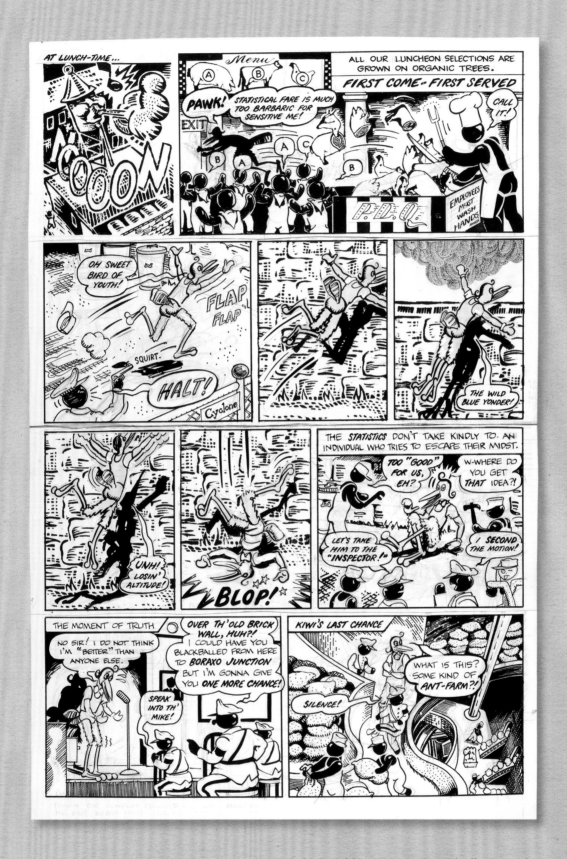

Pen and ink, rubber-stamp art, and silk screen | 20 × 30 inches

A surreal take on the real-world workplace, "Matriculation" reflects the idiosyncratic approach typical of Justin Green. The original pages are physically much larger than typical original comix art, and they are unusual in that they employ mixed media. Green's painfully autobiographical comic *Binky Brown Meets the Holy Virgin Mary* (1972) is regarded as a true classic with profound influence. Despite his high stature among colleagues, Green was not able to sustain a career in comics. Making his living primarily as a sign painter, he keeps a foot in comics by doing a monthly strip, *Sign Game,* for a sign-industry trade journal.

JUSTIN GREEN

"Zen Time," 1978

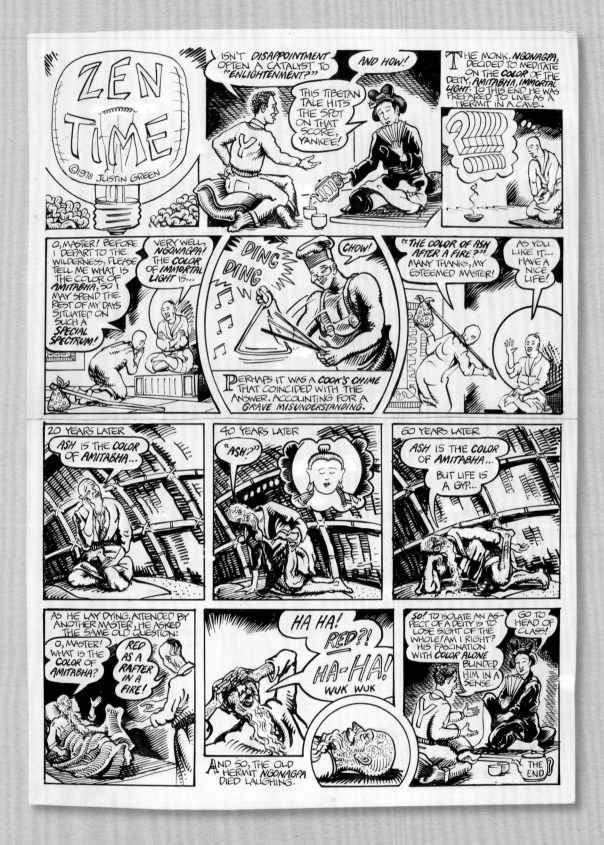

Pen and ink | 14¾ × 19 inches

Justin Green openly acknowledges his obsessive-compulsive disorder as an essential element in his artistic development. The influence of Surrealism is also clear in his work, which often focuses on the role of religion (Roman Catholicism in *Binky Brown Meets the Holy Virgin Mary*). In "Zen Time" the quest for personal enlightenment fatefully crosses swords with obsession.

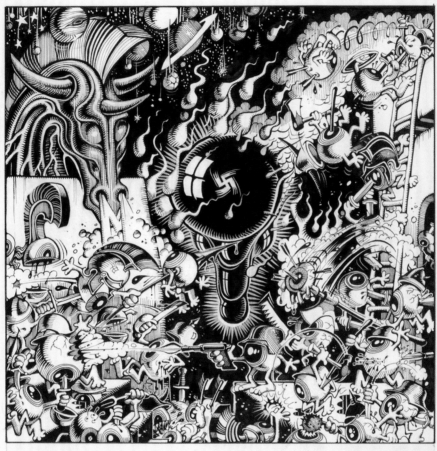

Brush, pen, and ink | 11 × 16 inches

Growing up in Southern California exposed Rick Griffin to the blossoming surf culture and led to his seminal cartoons in *Surfer* magazine, including an issue he guest edited that included contributions from Robert Crumb, Robert Williams, and S. Clay Wilson, among others. Griffin, who also created album covers and concert posters, distinguished himself from nearly all of his contemporaries through his conversion to Christianity, which he addressed in *Man from Utopia* (1970).

RICK GRIFFIN

Zap no. 2, inside front cover, 1968

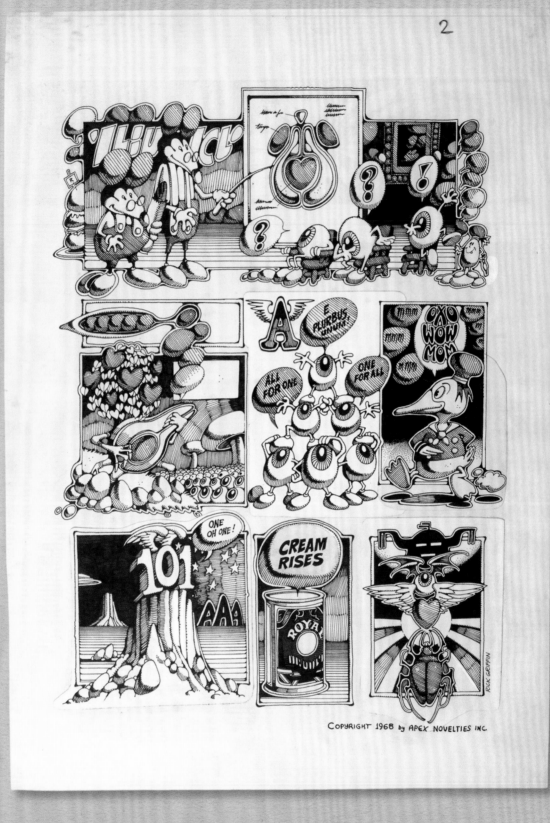

Brush, pen, and ink | 15 × 20 inches

Rick Griffin, like so many budding cartoonists of the post–World War II era, began by drawing icons of the new consumer culture in his native California: hot rods and surfers. By the late 1960s Griffin's memorable posters for rock shows at the Fillmore in San Francisco and his iconic album and other art for the Grateful Dead cemented his reputation as one of the most important visual influences on the period. His contributions to *Zap*, his first shown here, continued during his relatively short career, though his long interest in mysticism is clearly evident in his work.

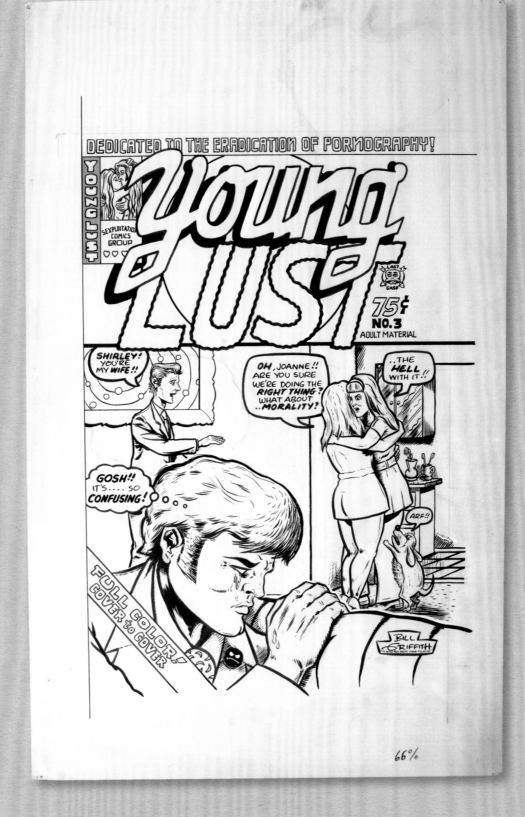

Brush, pen, and ink | 11 × 14 inches

In 1969, after meeting cartoonist Jay Kinney, Bill Griffith conceived the idea for *Young Lust,* a comic that would draw a deep contrast between the sexually liberated lifestyles emerging in the 1960s and the formally constrained mores of the 1950s. *Young Lust* offered a parody of traditional romance periodicals while also serving as a sex-based comic that would appeal to female readers—a rarity.

BILL GRIFFITH

Zippy Stories, cover, 1981

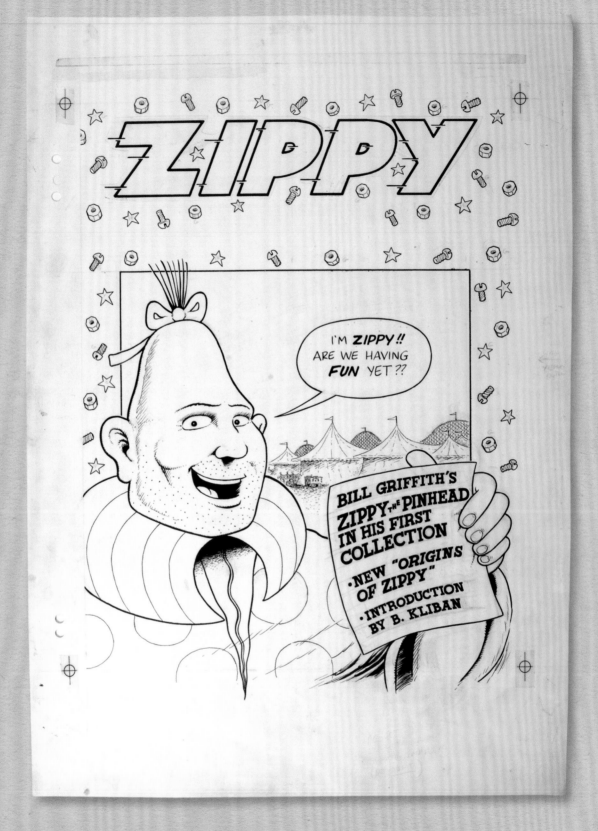

Pen and ink | 14 × 22 inches

"Zip the What-Is-It" was the name given to a sideshow pinhead (microcephalic) exhibited by Barnum & Bailey's Circus from 1864 to 1926. Bill Griffith's guileless Zippy the Pinhead was popularized in numerous underground comix titles before making the unprecedented transition from comix to daily newspapers. *Zippy* is today a King Features syndicated strip, where Zippy's naïve pronouncements and topical nonsequiturs, often with the cartoonist himself as straight man, provide offbeat insights for many. Zippy's signature phrase is, "Am I having fun yet?"

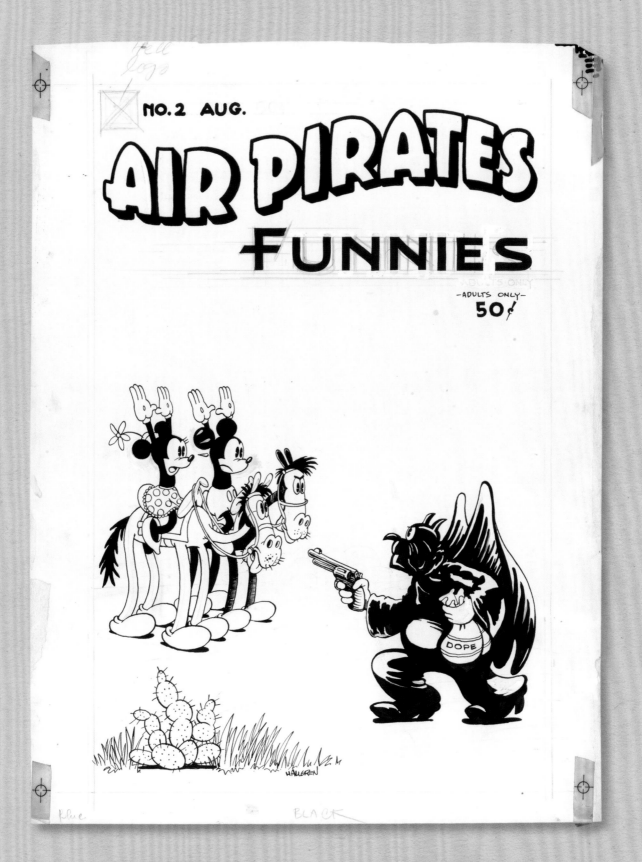

Brush, pen, and ink | 15 × 20 inches

In 1971, Gary Hallgren and several other artists, including Dan O'Neill, teamed up to produce two issues of *Air Pirates Funnies*. The comics contained risqué parody versions of Mickey and Minnie Mouse, which led to a highly publicized lawsuit with the Walt Disney Company. The artists ultimately lost in a unanimous U.S. Supreme Court showdown. Hallgren became a frequent contributor to *National Lampoon* magazine and has had a successful career as a freelance illustrator, including his work for a bestselling series of medical guides.

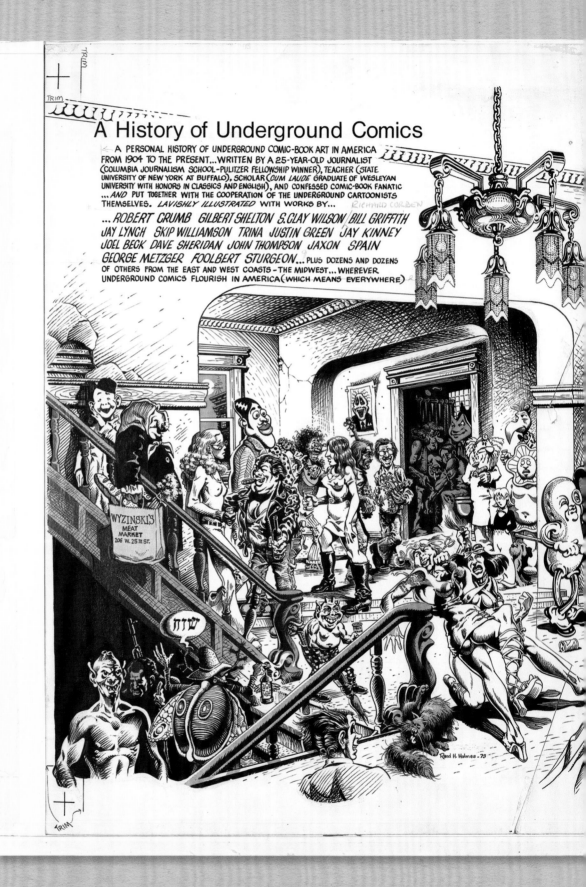

Brush and ink | 30 × 20 inches

A History of Underground Comics by Mark James Estren was published by Straight Arrow, an arm of *Rolling Stone*. Estren's book continues to be a basic source for anyone interested in comix. Rand Holmes, tapped for this plum cover assignment, drew a variety of the cartoonists' creations and guests interacting at a party gathering. Best known

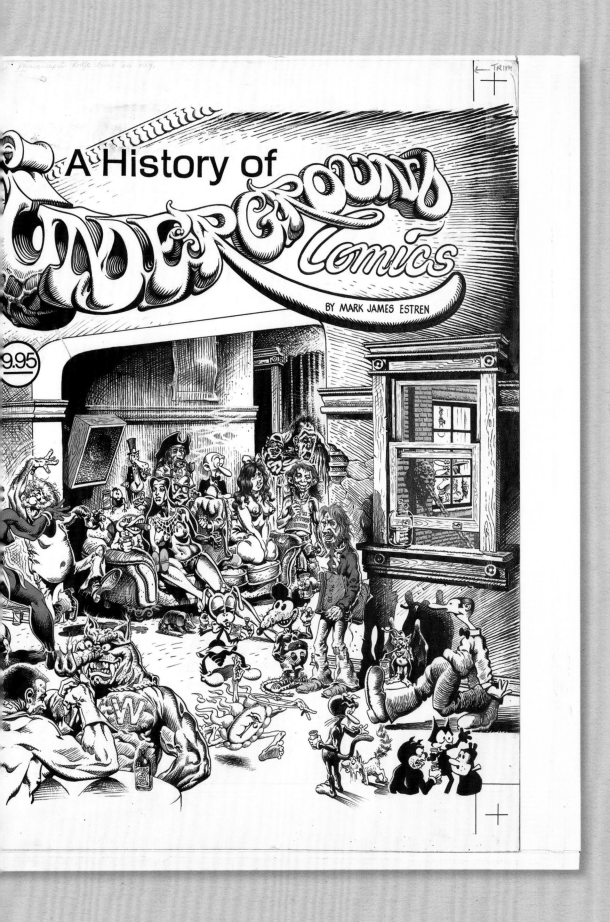

for his *Harold Hedd* series, Holmes abandoned the San Francisco scene early on to live in isolation on an island off British Columbia, but remained an important if long-distance member of the comix fraternity. For a complete identification key to the characters in this crowd, refer to the back endpaper.

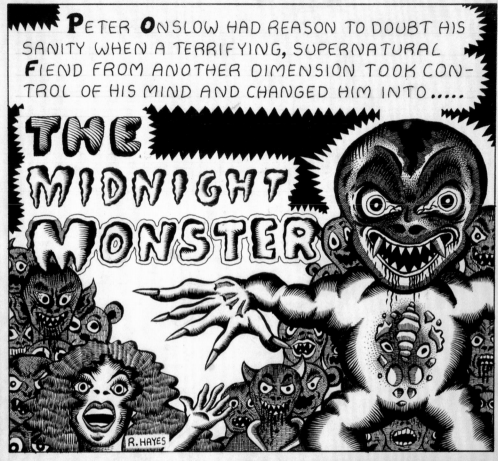

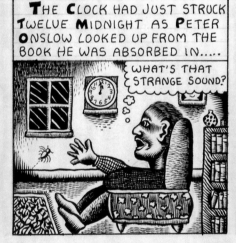 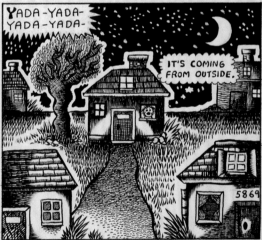

Pen and ink | 9 × 12½ inches

This splash page appeared in *Insect Fear* no. 3, published by the Print Mint in San Francisco. Rory Hayes's eccentric cartoons were popular among some of his more artistically accomplished colleagues. Sometimes called the "Grandma Moses of undergrounds" for his primitive folk style, Hayes's rendering of misogynistic fantasies and tortured teddy-bear archetypes made the comparison a limited one. A collection of Hayes's work, *Where Demented Wented*, was recently published by Fantagraphics.

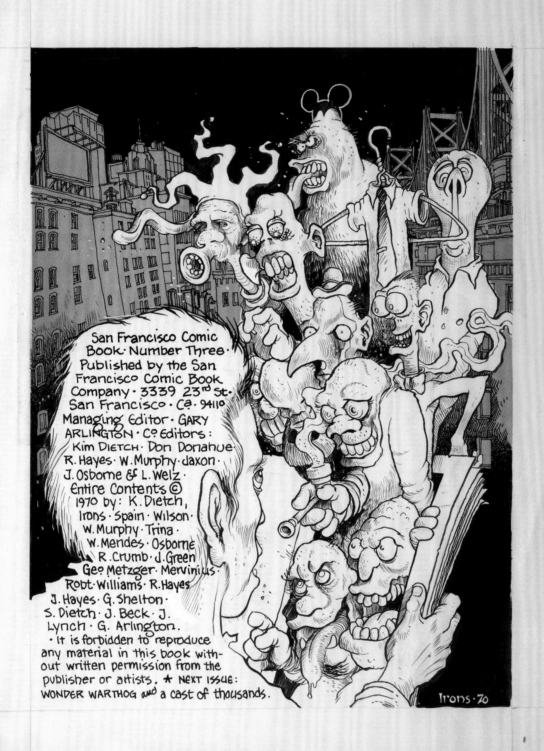

San Francisco Comic
Book· Number Three·
Published by the San
Francisco Comic Book
Company· 3339 23rd St·
San Francisco· Ca· 94110·
Managing Editor· GARY
ARLINGTON· Co-Editors:
Kim Dietch· Don Donahue·
R. Hayes· W. Murphy· daxon·
J. Osborne & L. Welz·
Entire Contents ©
1970 by: K. Dietch,
Irons· Spain· Wilson·
W. Murphy· Trina·
W. Mendes· Osborne·
R. Crumb· J. Green·
Geo. Metzger· Mervinius·
Robt· Williams· R. Hayes·
J. Hayes· G. Shelton·
S. Dietch· J. Beck· J.
Lynch· G. Arlington.
· It is forbidden to reproduce
any material in this book with-
out written permission from the
publisher or artists. ★ NEXT ISSUE:
WONDER WARTHOG and a cast of thousands.

Irons·70

Pen and ink with Zip-A-Tone | 11 × 14 inches

Born in Philadelphia, Greg Irons headed west and by 1967 was doing psychedelic posters for Bill Graham at the Fillmore. Irons was prolific in comix, contributing to titles such as *Yellow Dog, Dr. Wertham's Comix & Stories, Slow Death, Deviant Slice,* and *Dope Comix.* His magnum opus may have been *The Legion of Charlies* (with writer Tom Veitch), which compared Charles Manson's grotesqueries with those of Vietnam villain Lt. William Calley. This indicia-page illustration anticipates that at least some readers may have a trippy experience with the book's contents.

GREG IRONS

Slow Death Funnies no. 1, cover, 1970

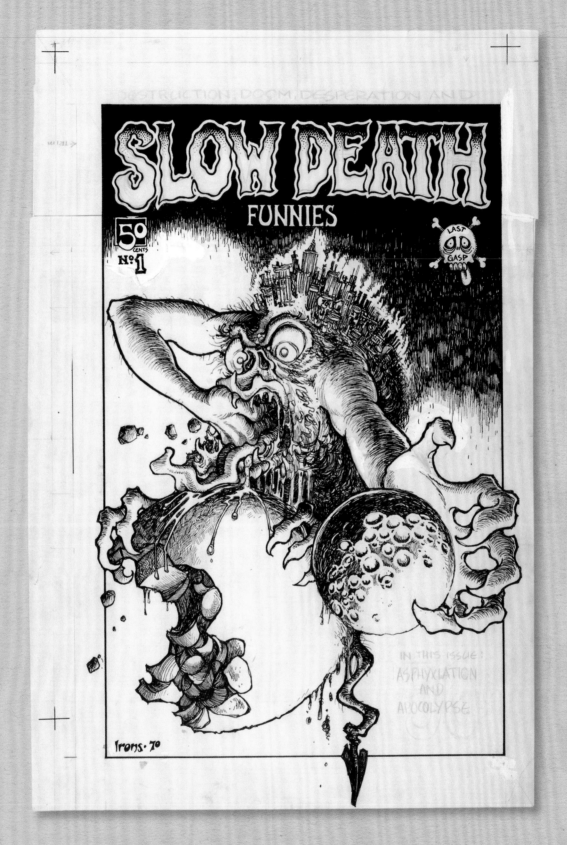

Brush, pen, and ink | 12 × 19 inches

In Greg Irons's graphic depiction of ecological disaster, a skyscraper-encrusted Earth consumes itself. The first issue of *Slow Death Funnies* featured contributions by Dave Sheridan, Gilbert Shelton, and other artists. The anthology was Last Gasp's entry into comix publishing, led by environmental activist Ron Turner. Later in his abbreviated career, Greg Irons became a celebrated tattoo artist.

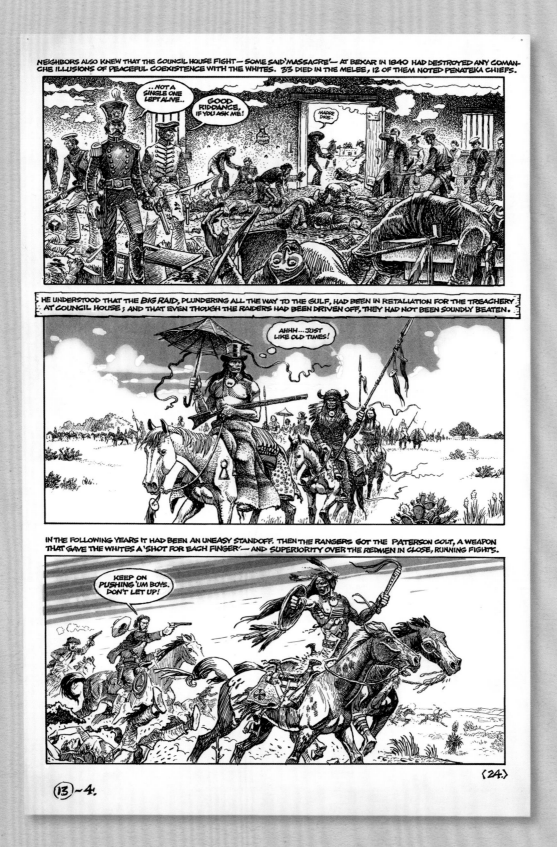

Pen and ink with Zip-A-Tone | 11 ¼ × 17 inches

Jack Jackson's self-published *God Nose* (1964) is regarded by many as the first underground comic. A founding member of the Rip Off Press crew originating in Austin, Texas, "Jaxon" initially produced E.C.-influenced horror comics for the San Francisco-based company. Before long he returned home to create historical comics and, specifically, comics about Texas history. This page is from *Comanche Moon*, an account of Cynthia Ann Parker, a young girl captured in 1836 by a band of Texas Comanches, and her half Indian son Quanah, who eventually became the tribe's last chief.

JACK JACKSON (JAXON)
Portrait of Quanah Parker, 1985

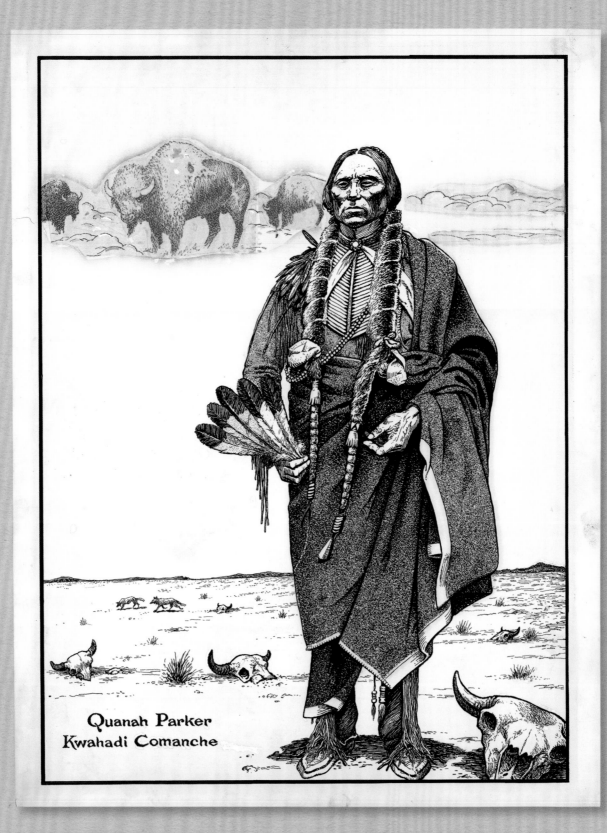

Quanah Parker
Kwahadi Comanche

Pen and ink with Zip-A-Tone | 14 ⅝ × 18 ¾ inches

Jackson combined his distinctive graphic ability with his deep knowledge of Texas's past to create *Los Tejanos, Lost Cause, El Alamo, Secret of San Saba,* and *Comanche Moon,* graphic novels embraced by historians and comics fans alike. The lesser-known *Long Shadows: Indian Leaders Standing in the Path of Manifest Destiny, 1600–1900,* featured portraits and short biographies of twenty-seven important American chiefs. Shown here is Jackson's portrait of Quanah Parker, the chief whose life during the final battles of the Western frontier was dramatically chronicled in *Comanche Moon.*

JAY KINNEY

"Say! Whatever Happened to the Counterculture?" 1980

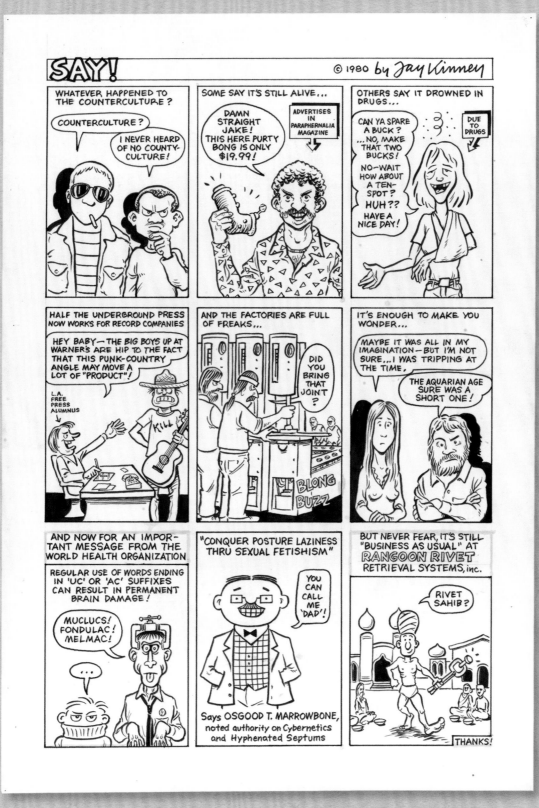

Brush, pen, and ink | 10 × 15 inches

In this bittersweet reflection on the fate of the counterculture from *Dope Comix* no. 4 (1980), the artist concludes that the hopes and dreams from that period are over. Kinney was part of the first wave of artists who came to define comix, as an early fanzine artist and contributor to *Bijou Funnies* beginning with its first issue in 1968. Jay Kinney's career included extensive comix work as well as serving as an editor for a variety of periodicals including *Anarchy Comics*, *Young Lust*, *Co-Evolution Quarterly*, and *Gnosis*.

Denis Kitchen, Don Glassford, Jay Lynch, Jim Mitchell, Wendel Pugh, Bruce Walthers, Skip Williamson

"Group Self-portrait," 1971

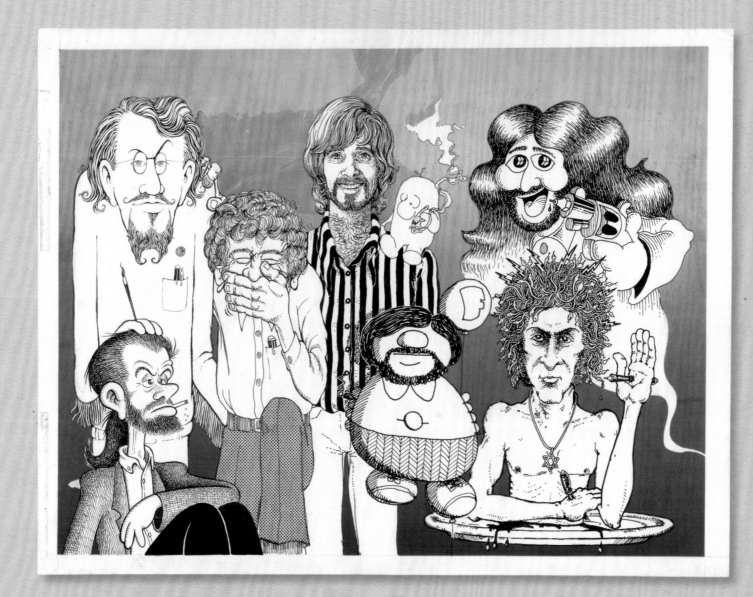

Brush, pen, and ink with Zip-A-Tone | 11¾ × 9¼ inches

The primary base for underground comix was in the San Francisco Bay Area, but the second-biggest pocket was in America's heartland. This chummy group portrait depicts the core Midwestern underground cartoonists. Back row, left to right: Denis Kitchen (*Mom's Homemade Comics*), Don Glassford (*Deep 3-D Comix*), Jim Mitchell (*Smile*), and Skip Williamson (*Snappy Sammy Smoot*). Front row, left to right: Jay Lynch (*Nard 'n Pat*), Bruce Walthers (*O.K. Comics*), and Wendel Pugh (*Googiewaumer Comics*). Lynch and Williamson worked in Chicago at the time, while the other five were Milwaukeeans. This jam was created for a 1971 *Funnyworld* article on underground comix. The Michael Barrier-run periodical was devoted to measuring contemporary cartoonists and animators against traditional artistic standards.

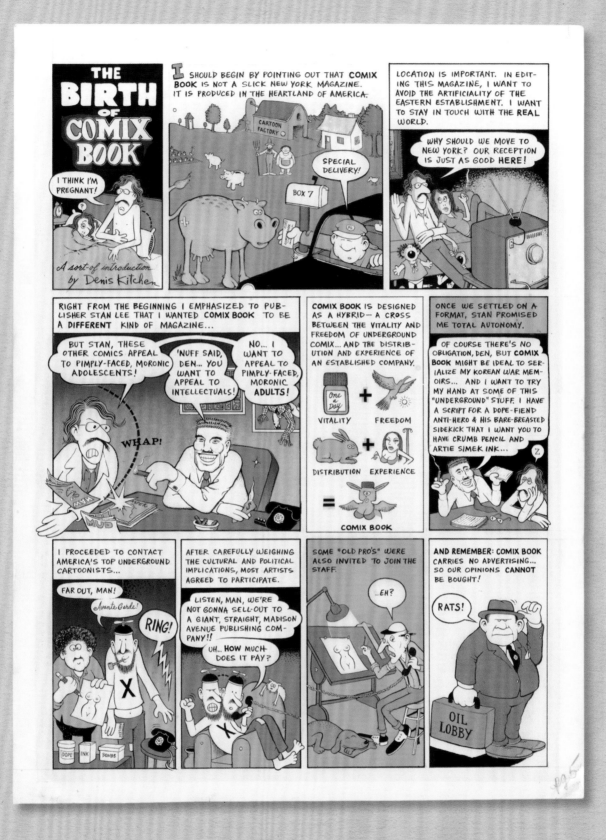

Brush, pen, and ink with Zip-A-Tone | 11 × 15¼ inches

Editor-artist Denis Kitchen's tongue-in-cheek origin story of Marvel's hybrid underground/newsstand magazine appeared in the debut issue of *Comix Book*. The experimental magazine was driven by writer-editor Stan Lee's desire to tap into the energy of underground comix and many cartoonists' desire to stop starving after the comix-market crash of '73. The heartland farm in the second panel was Kitchen's Wisconsin homestead. Lee is unflatteringly depicted as Spider-Man's nemesis J. Jonah Jameson, though underground cartoonists are not immune from skewering here either.

Denis Kitchen

Bizarre Sex no. 1, cover, 1972; Opposite: *Bugle-American* no. 216, fifth anniversary cover, 1975

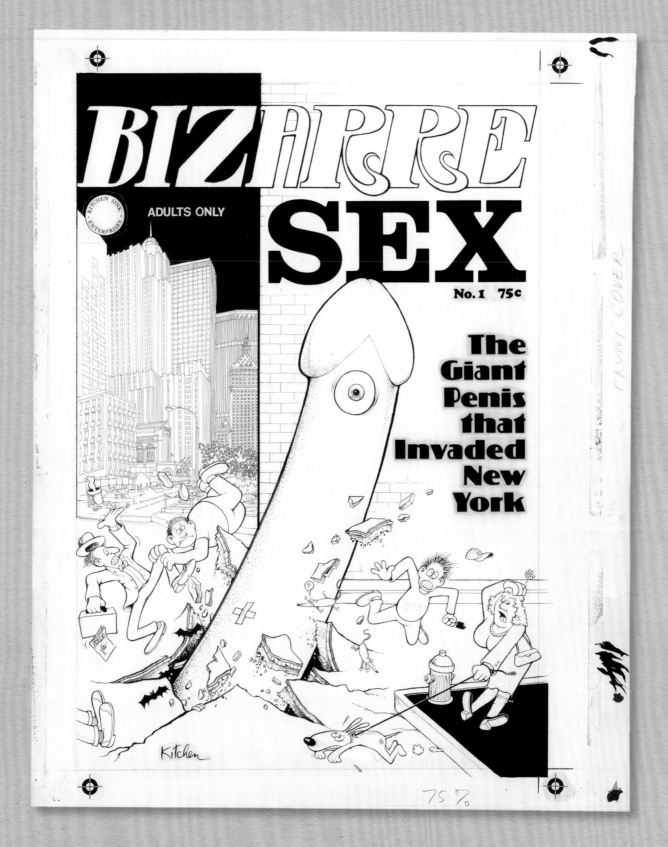

Pen and ink | 14 × 16¾ inches

1972 was the high-water mark for sales of underground comix, and one of the best sellers for Kitchen Sink Press was *Bizarre Sex*. The vision for "The Giant Penis that Invaded New York" came to the cartoonist during a memorable acid trip, though many purchasers later complained that there was no story to go with the provocative cover. Editor Dave Schreiner used to joke that this cover represented Kitchen's "seminal work."

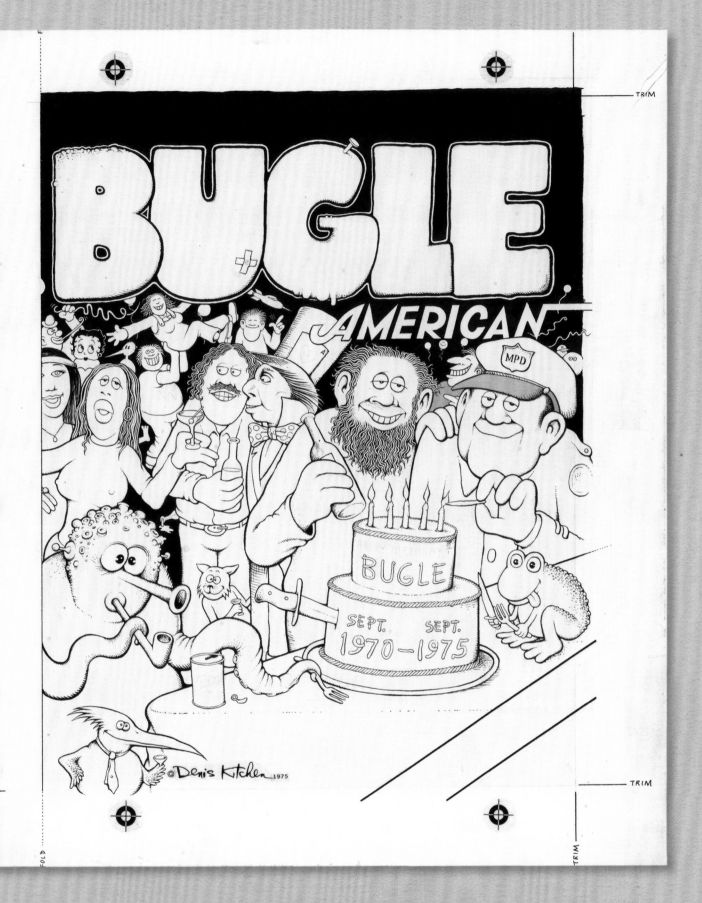

Pen and ink | 11¼ × 13 inches

In addition to his comix company, Kitchen cofounded the weekly *Bugle-American* in 1970, Wisconsin's longest-running (seven years) underground/alternative newspaper. Later shortened to the *Bugle*, the paper uniquely featured full pages of homegrown comic strips, syndicated to fifty other alternative and college papers. Kitchen and other cartoonists often created covers too. This one, printed in rare full-color, celebrated the paper's fifth anniversary.

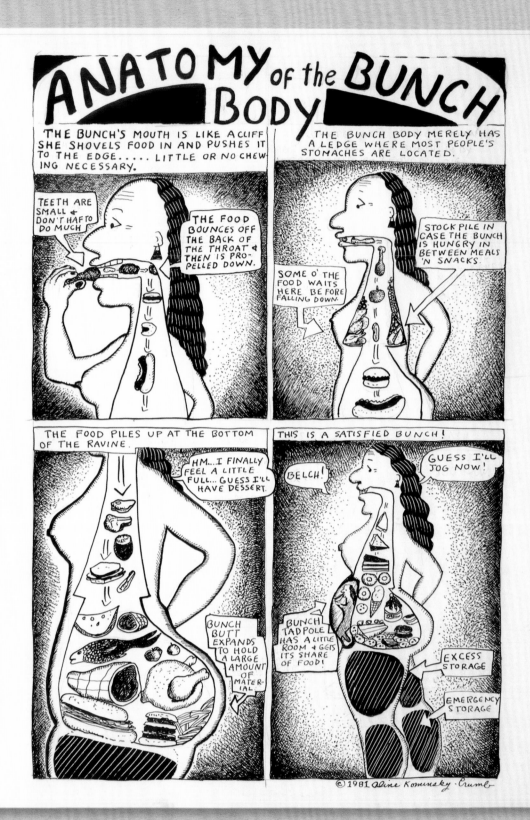

Pen and ink | 12 × 13 inches

In this page from *Power Pak* no. 2 (1981), Aline Kominsky Crumb (affectionately known as "The Bunch") combines her trademarks: an acerbic self-deprecating humor, Jewish shtick, and frank autobiography. Her periodic jams with husband Robert Crumb have appeared in the *New Yorker* and their own *Dirty Laundry Comics*, and her solo work has been collected in *Need More Love: A Graphic Memoir*.

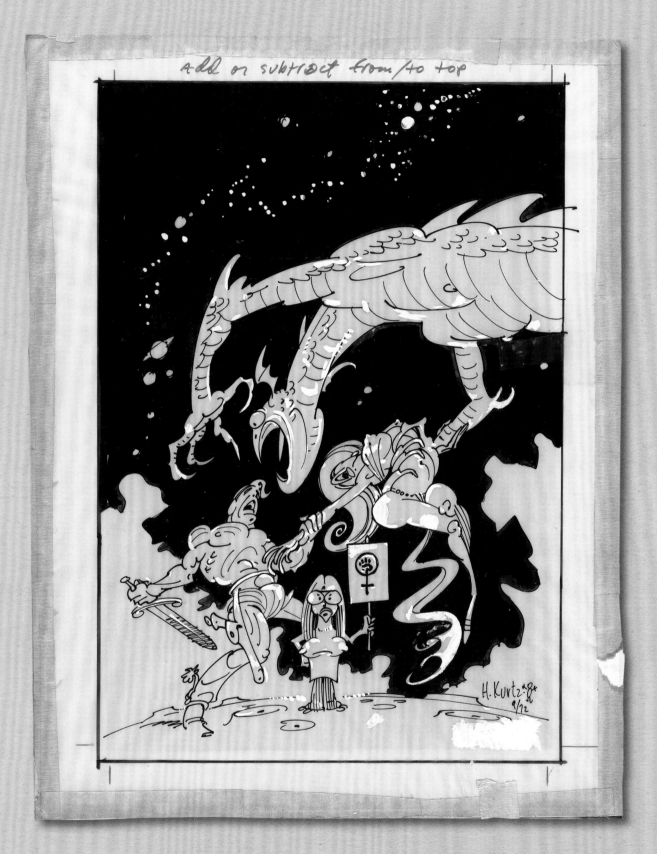

Pen and ink | 11¼ × 14½ inches

Harvey Kurtzman profoundly influenced the underground cartoonists as well as many readers of his groundbreaking publications *MAD*, *Humbug*, *Trump*, and *Help!*. R. Crumb, Gilbert Shelton, Jay Lynch, Skip Williamson, and Joel Beck all received their first national exposure in the latter magazine (not to mention Gloria Steinem and Terry Gilliam). Like Will Eisner, Kurtzman was not bounded by his own generation; he reached out to new ideas and to new cartoonists. Here Flash Gordon, a comics icon of the thirties and forties, finds that rescuing hapless, barely clad women has become more complicated in the seventies.

BOBBY LONDON

"Dirty Duck: Evils of Hashish" 1973

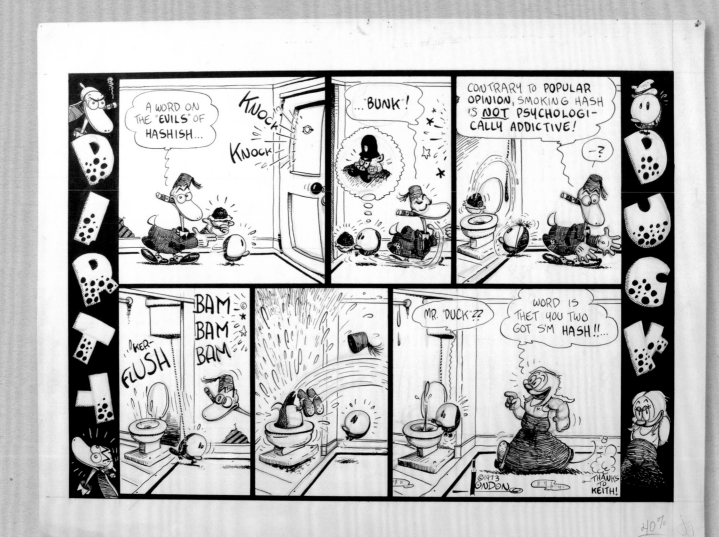

Pen and ink | 19 × 14 inches

Bobby London, along with ringleader Dan O'Neill, was part of the notorious Air Pirates crew. London's throwback art echoes the style of George Herriman (*Krazy Kat*), while his lead character takes some cues from comedian Groucho Marx. Dirty Duck cavorts through a landscape reminiscent of *Krazy Kat*'s Coconino County, except that drugs and sex are prevalent. After underground comix faded, London drew the daily *Popeye* newspaper strip for six years, until a gag alluding to abortion caused King Features to fire him in 1992.

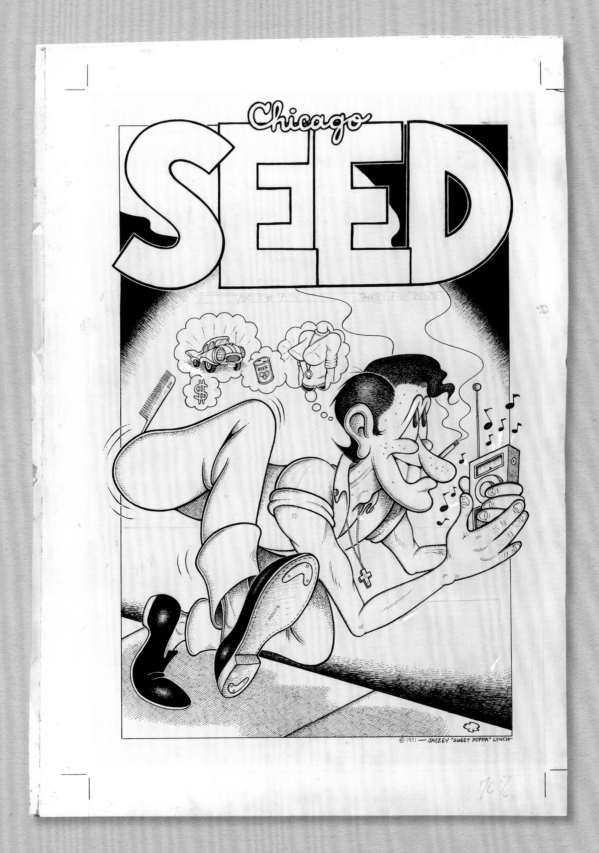

Pen and ink | 13¼ × 18¾ inches

Thousands of politically charged underground newspapers appeared and soon disappeared in the decade following the 1964 debut of the pioneering *Los Angeles Free Press*. The *Seed*, edited by Abe Peck, was a Chicago underground newspaper published from 1967 to 1971. It featured some of the most interesting comic art of the period. The politically correct staff of the *Seed* rejected Jay Lynch's 1971 fifties hipster cover because of the "emphasis on breasts," but his colleague Denis Kitchen happily accepted it as a cover for Wisconsin's alternative paper, the *Bugle*.

Jay Lynch

Snarf no. 2, cover, 1972; Opposite: *Dope Comix* no. 3, cover, 1979

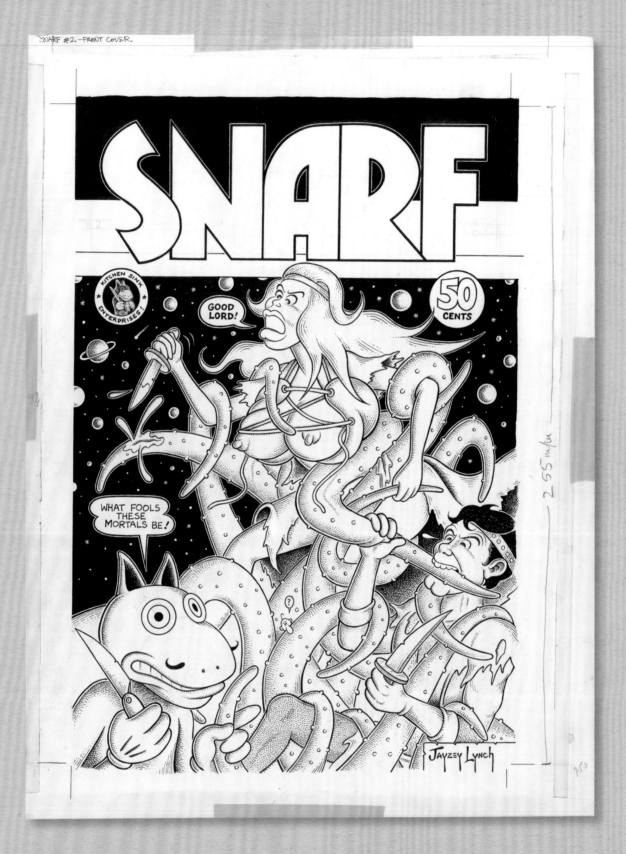

Pen and ink | 13½ × 18 inches

Science fiction? Sexist? Freudian? Existential? This popular underground humor anthology featured an eclectic content mix, so a bafflingly surreal cover such as this effort by "Jayzey" Lynch would not have deterred its largely hippie customer base. Lynch's best-known creations were the human-cat duo, Nard 'n Pat (Pat the Cat was the smart one), stars of the Lynch-edited *Bijou Funnies* series and two solo issues.

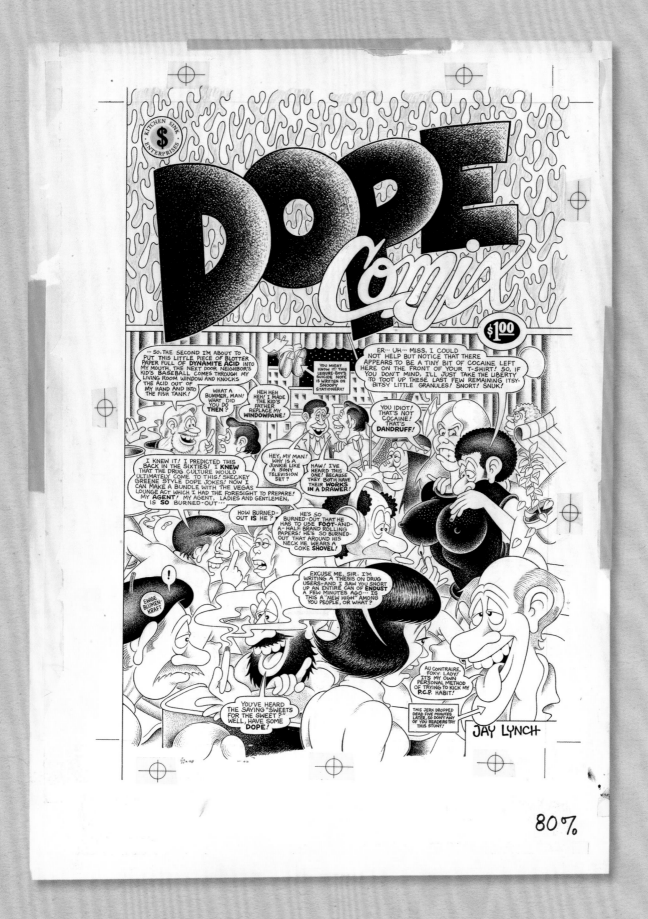

Pen and ink | 14 × 18 inches

Perhaps no title better captures the ethos of the 1960s and 1970s than *Dope Comix*. The microscopic detail of this cover reflects the artist's obsessive attention, aided by a pinpoint "triple zero" Rapidograph pen. Though the title suggests otherwise, a number of contributors took an antidrug stance. Jay Lynch (by this time a drug teetotaler) here reflects his jaded view of the 1970s drug scene. After undergrounds peaked as a publishing phenomenon, he developed a new following, creating much of the art and ideas behind the Topps trading-card series *Garbage Pail Kids* and *Wacky Packages*.

JIM MITCHELL

"Jim Mitchell's Pro Junior Comix," 1971

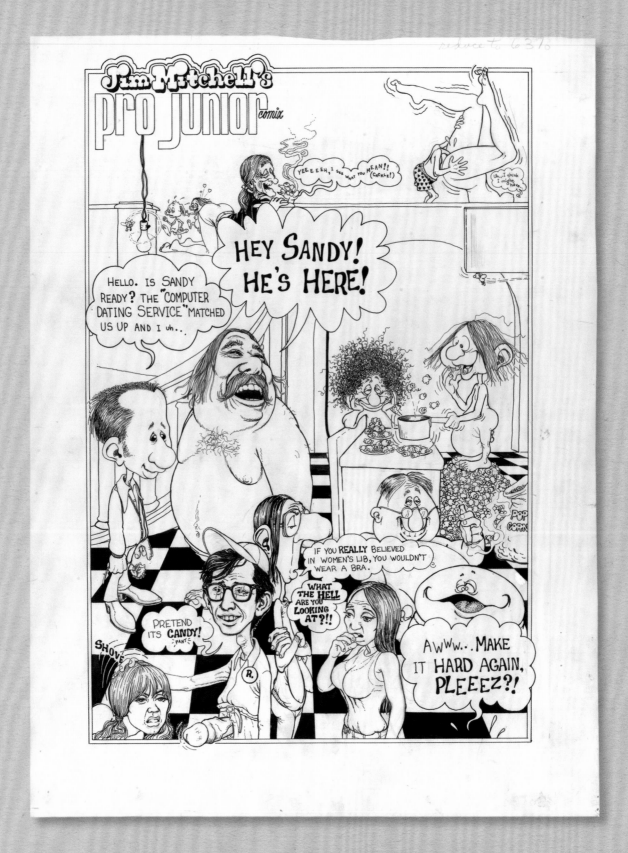

Pen and ink | each 13¼ × 17½ inches

Jim Mitchell's work appeared in *Teen-age Horizons of Shangri-La, Mom's Homemade Comics,* and his own *Smile* series. Reverse-eyed Pro Junior was a communally owned character, defying conventional notions of trademark. Mitchell's versatile style ranged from the very simple line drawings of *Smile* to nuanced caricatures. The fellow saying, "Pretend it's candy," is R. Crumb, and the sub-scene parodies his infamously prosecuted "Joe Blow" story in *Zap* no. 4. Mitchell's career was interrupted in the seventies when he served several years in a Mexican prison for drug charges.

Reduce to 61%
THAT POPCORN SMELLS REEEEALLY GOOD!!
HEY PA! CAN I BORROW YOUR TEETH FOR A FEW MINUTES?
SIPH?
OH BLAST! I SPECIFICALLY ORDERED A TALL ONE!!
EVER WONDERED WHAT THE GUYS THAT DRAW THESE THINGS MUST BE LIKE?
WEIRD!
MAKE IT HARD!!
©1971
YUMMY NUMMY!
Crunch!

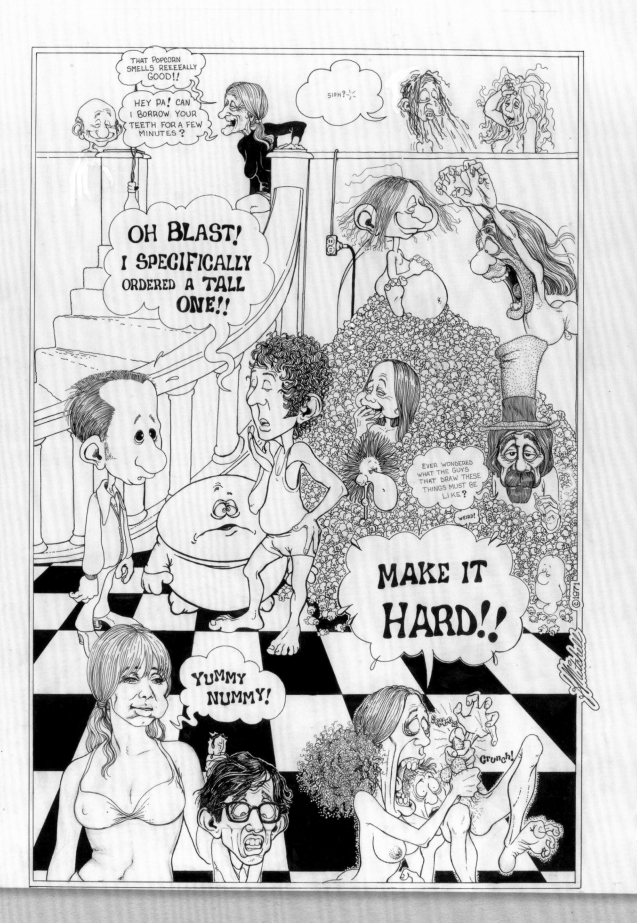

VICTOR MOSCOSO

"Artist & Model Comics," 1978

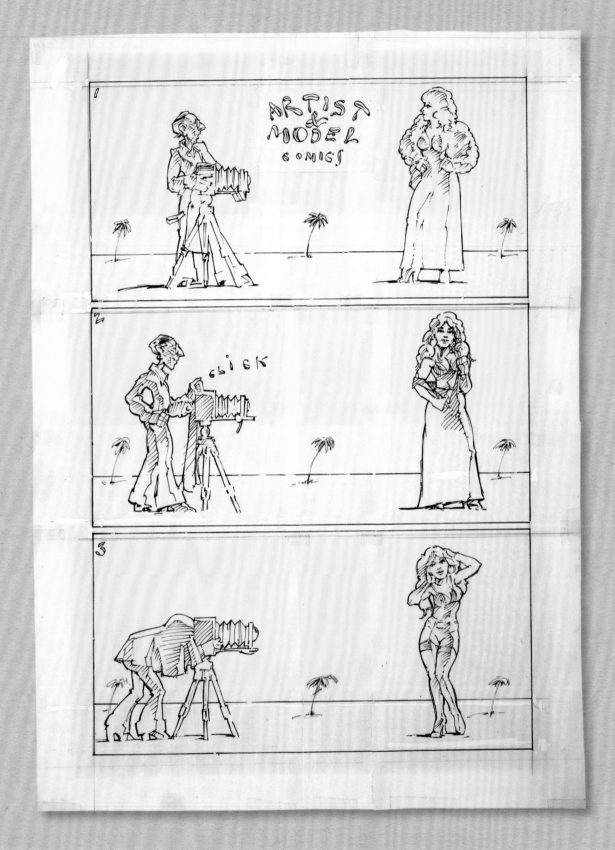

Pen and ink | 10 × 15 inches

R. Crumb's groundbreaking debut issue of *Zap* was printed by Charles Pymell, a Beat writer who shared a house with Allen Ginsberg and Neal Cassady. After two solo issues, Crumb unselfishly invited other artists to join the valuable *Zap* brand. S. Clay Wilson, Robert Williams, Spain Rodriguez, Gilbert Shelton, and Rick Griffin (and, later, Paul Mavrides) became associated with *Zap*, in addition to Victor Moscoso. Like Griffin, Moscoso was perhaps even better known for the psychedelic art and concert posters he produced for the Fillmore and other clients.

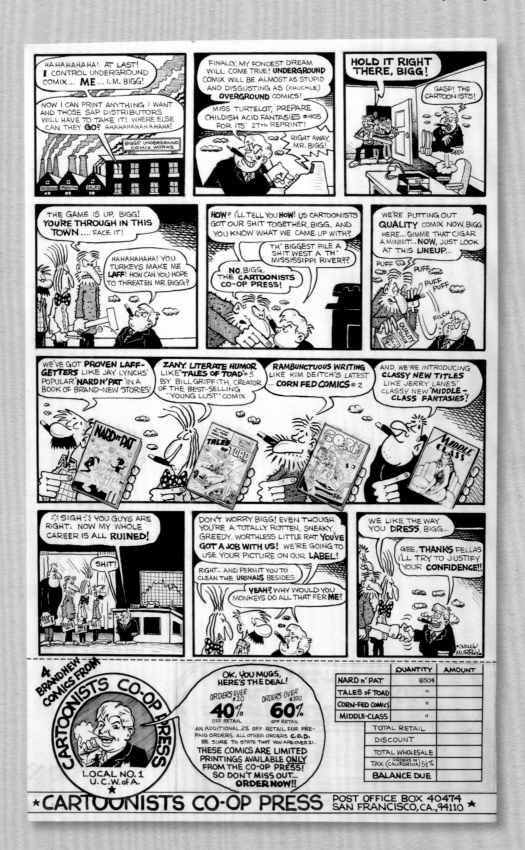

Pen and ink | 13 × 20½ inches

In the summer of 1973, Bill Griffith, Kim Deitch, Jerry Lane, and Jay Lynch had new comix ready to go but had trouble finding a publisher in the fallout of the Supreme Court decision that left questions of obscenity up to local governments. Thus was born the short-lived Cartoonists Co-Op Press, which argued that an artist co-op could net artists a greater share of revenues. In his own *Flamed-Out Funnies* and appearances in comix anthologies, Willy Murphy showed himself to be one of the funniest cartoonists emerging from undergrounds. Murphy's goal was to be comic, not just draw them.

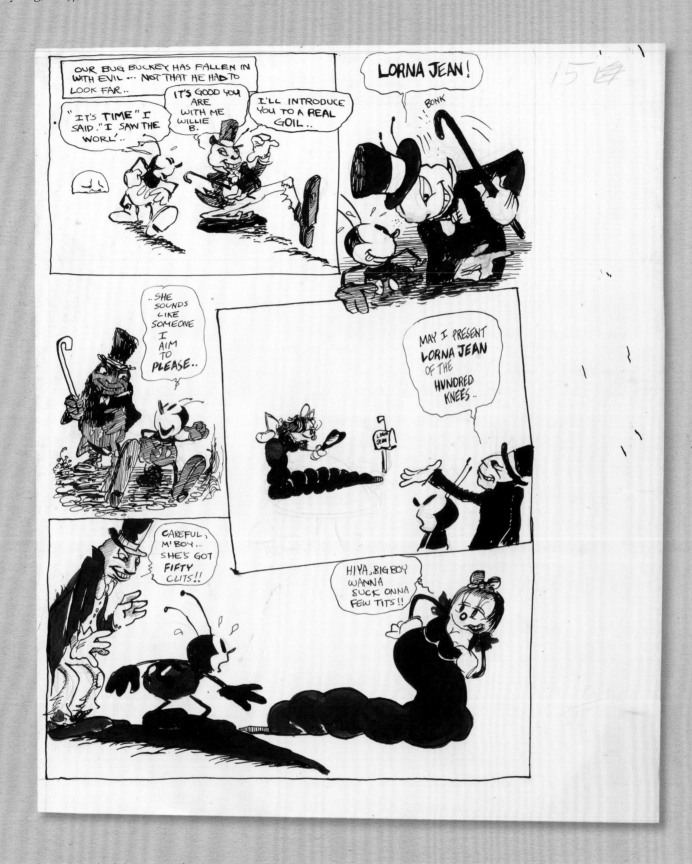

Brush, pen, and ink | 11 × 17 inches

Dan O'Neill founded the Air Pirates, a group that included Shary Flenniken, Bobby London, Gary Hallgren, and Ted Richards. The group released two issues of *Air Pirates Funnies* in 1971, opening a celebrated legal battle with the Walt Disney Company. Individual Pirates mined the styles of past masters of comic art. The sexual nature of "Buckey Bug" suggests what Disney found objectionable in *Air Pirates Funnies*, besides mere copyright and trademark issues.

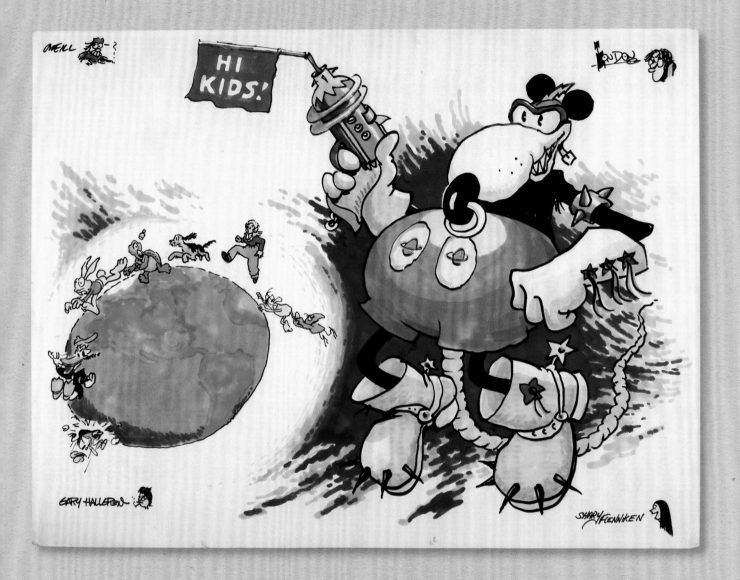

Colored markers | 20 × 15 inches

Four of the five artists comprising the Air Pirates depict Mickey Mouse as an ominous galactic threat in this playful jam. The Disney organization is an obvious target for satirists, despite the company's litigious reputation. Dan O'Neill led the charge in the early seventies, taking Mickey and Minnie into the realms of sex and recreational drug use, which prompted Disney to sue—O'Neill's goal. Over the next decade, Disney's lawyers spent more than two million dollars to eventually successfully suppress the cartoonists for trademark and copyright violations. The artists' characters fleeing Mickey are (top to free fall): O'Neill's Odd Bodkins, Flenniken's Trots and Bonnie, Hallgren's Tortoise and Hare, and London's Dirty Duck (and Weevil). The artist's signatures are accompanied by mini self-caricatures.

JIM OSBORNE
"Vultura," 1971

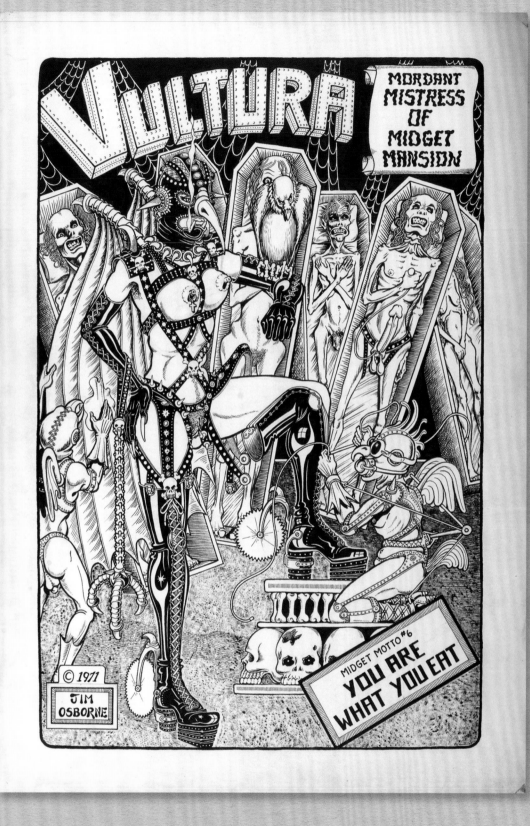

Pen and ink | 17 × 23 inches

Horror was a staple of comic books in the early 1950s (when many future underground artists first collected comics), and its graphic violence was instrumental in psychiatrist Dr. Fredric Wertham's campaign, which led to the industry's self-censoring Comics Code. Jim Osborne's "Vultura" added an over-the-top fetishistic necrophilia to the already creepy genre. Another Texas-born cartoonist who moved to San Francisco, Osborne contributed to titles such as *Bijou Funnies*, *Arcade*, *Insect Fear*, *Felch*, and *Sleazy Scandals of the Silver Screen* before abruptly leaving the field in the mid-1970s.

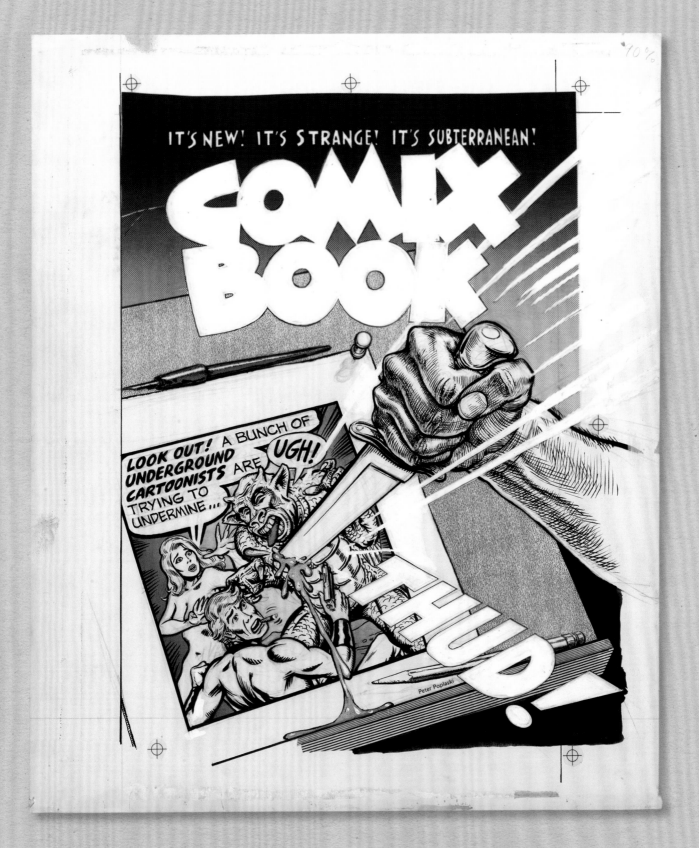

Brush, pen, and ink with Zip-A-Tone | 13¼ × 16 inches

Underground comix were hit by a double whammy in 1973. A Supreme Court decision on obscenity combined with a market glut drove publishers and artists to the brink. Stan Lee convinced Denis Kitchen to package *Comix Book* for Marvel Comics, introducing the underground to the mainstream. Peter Poplaski's cover for the debut issue dramatically announces a distinction between traditional comics and the new breed. The first to give creators copyright ownership and return original art, *Comix Book* opened a Pandora's box for mainstream comics and their creator rights.

PETER POPLASKI

Corporate Crime Comics no. 2, cover, 1979

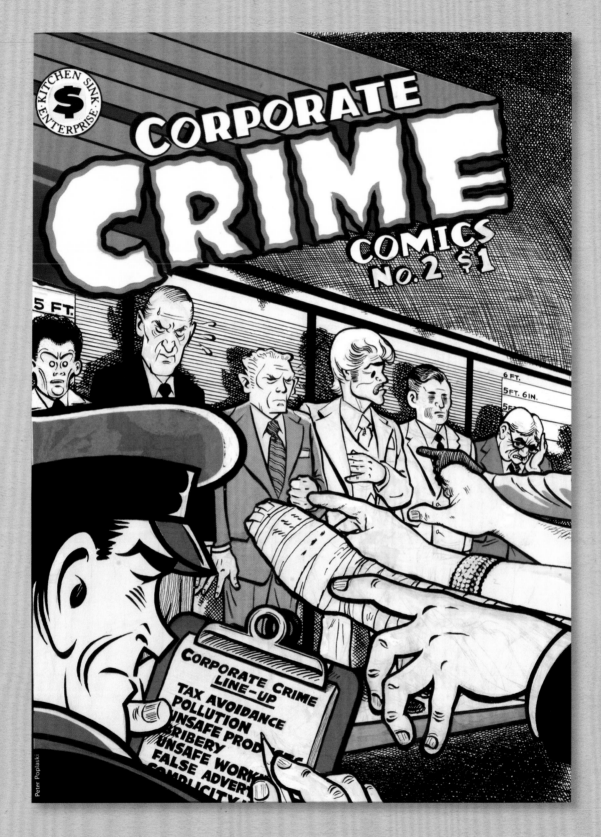

Brush, pen, and ink with Zip-A-Tone | 15½ × 19½ inches

Corporate Crime, edited by Leonard Rifas, turned traditional crime comics on their head, replacing bank robbers and murderers with white-collar criminals. Peter Poplaski, a versatile artist and expert mimic, here riffs on Chester Gould's *Dick Tracy* style with corporate criminal Alfred Krupp, second from left in the police lineup. Poplaski has more recently assembled definitive books on Robert Crumb (*The R. Crumb Coffee Table Art Book* and *The R. Crumb Handbook*) and collaborated on Will Eisner's final book (*Expressive Anatomy*).

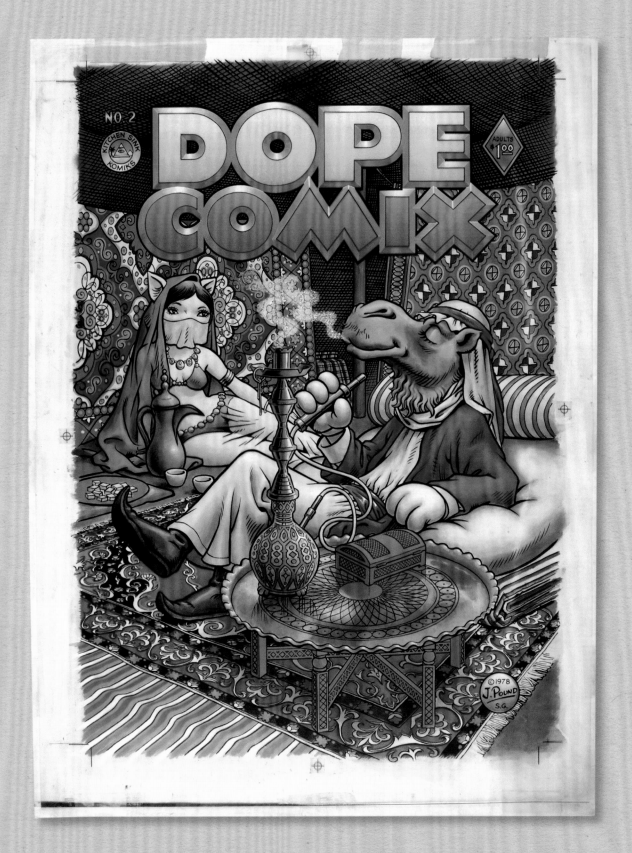

Brush, ink, and gouache | 16 × 22 inches

The camel smoking a hookah brings to mind a certain cigarette brand, but here the creature is blissful and in control, as the female harem suggests. The rich detail in the Oriental carpet, hookah, and tapestry lends a meditative quality to the image, from a concept by Steve Garris, which explains the cover's secondary popularity as a poster. John Pound later became famous for his cultish work on the *Garbage Pail Kids* for Topps, a trading-card series that also involved Art Spiegelman and Jay Lynch.

HARVEY PEKAR, ROBERT CRUMB

"Miracle Rabbis," 1982

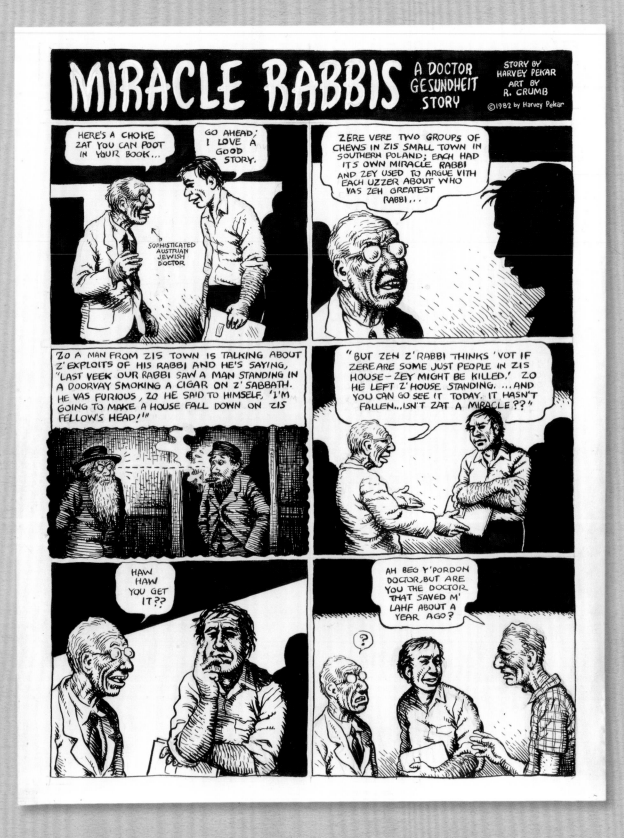

Pen and ink | each 23¾ × 29¼ inches

This collaboration between the writer and artist, "A Doctor Gesundheit Story," was for Harvey Pekar's famed *American Splendor*. R. Crumb and Pekar originally met as fellow collectors of 78-rpm records. The sometimes painfully autobiographical stories in *American Splendor* brought real life, or at least Harvey Pekar's tortured and sometimes tedious life, to the comics in a way that had few predecessors. His series inspired the 2003 *American Splendor* film, in which both Pekar and Crumb were portrayed by actors (Paul Giamatti and James Urbaniak, respectively).

MIRACLE RABBIS — P. 2
NO, I'M ZORRY, ZAT'S NOT ME...
HE HASN'T SAVED A LIFE IN YEARS.
WELL, THIS DOCTOR WAS ABOUT YORE HEIGHT AN' HE HAD GLASSES AN' WHITE HAIR, SO AH THOUGHT...
NO, YOU MUST BE MISTAKEN, SIR... I CAN'T TAKE Z'CREDIT FOR ZIS.
ACTUALLY HE AIN'T A DOCTOR AT ALL; HE'S A GOOD-HUMOR MAN.
WELL, AH COULDA SWORN... 'COURSE AH WUZ UNDER AN ANESTHETIC AT THE TAHM, SO MAYBE...
ZO ANYVAY, HERE'S ANUZZER STORY~~

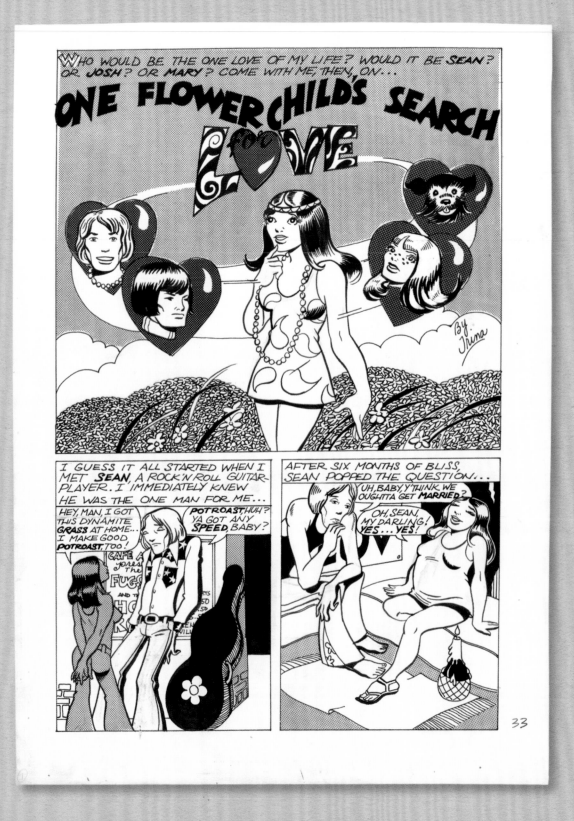

Brush, pen, and ink with Zip-A-Tone | each 12 × 17 inches

This tongue-in-cheek story of archetypal Haight-Ashbury hippies (sometimes called flower children by the media) was influenced by the fifties romance comics that Trina Robbins devoured as a young fan. A pioneer in many ways, especially being a woman in a field dominated by men, her *It Ain't Me Babe* was the first underground with a feminist theme. Robbins also pushed the boundaries of gender and sexuality with *Wet Satin*, an anthology of "women's erotic fantasies" that she edited and contributed to. Her books, *A Century of Women Cartoonists*, *The Great Women Super Heroes*, and *Women and Comics* are essential resources for scholars in the field.

BUT ONE DAY MY WORLD COLLAPSED...
RUDY! WHAT IS THE MEANING OF THIS?
TAMI! I CAN EXPLAIN EVERYTHING!
UH, WREN, THIS IS MY OLD LADY, TAMI, WHO'S BEEN STAYING IN THE CITY FOR A WHILE! TAMI, IT'S NOT WHAT YOU THINK - WREN AND I ARE JUST FRIENDS...
RUDY WASN'T "THE ONE", EITHER...
JUST FRIENDS!?! OH ≥SOB≤ RUDY, HOW COULD YOU?
WREN! WAIT!
ANGUS FOUND ME SOBBING MY HEART OUT IN THE VEGETABLE PATCH...
NOW, NOW, LITTLE BIRD! TELL UNCLE ANGUS!
OH ≥SOB≤ RUDY!
THE WORDS POURED FROM MY TREMBLING LIPS...
...AND NOW HE SAYS WE'RE JUST FRIENDS! OH, ANGUS, WHAT SHOULD I DO?
LET ME THINK...
I KNOW! LETS YOU AND ME AND RUDY AND TAMI ALL TAKE ACID TOGETHER AND SEE WHAT HAPPENS!
OH, ANGUS, HOW CLEVER YOU ARE!
36

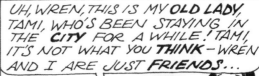

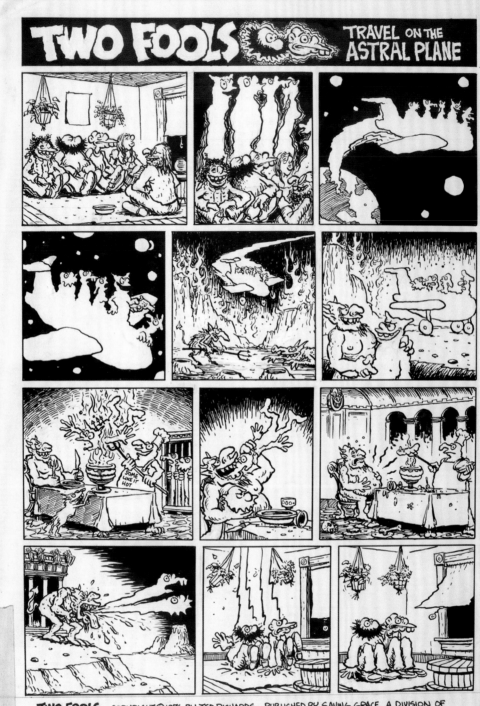

Pen and ink | 12¼ × 18½ inches

In this page from *Two Fools*, a book done in collaboration with the late Willy Murphy and others, Ted Richards tweaks an aspect of the New Age movement, while revealing that some souls are undesirable even to Satan. Richards was a member of the Air Pirates crew as well as the Rip Off Press gang. His character Ezekiel Wolf (aka E. Z. Wolf) evolved from the Pirates' efforts to mine early comics strips for styles and inspiration.

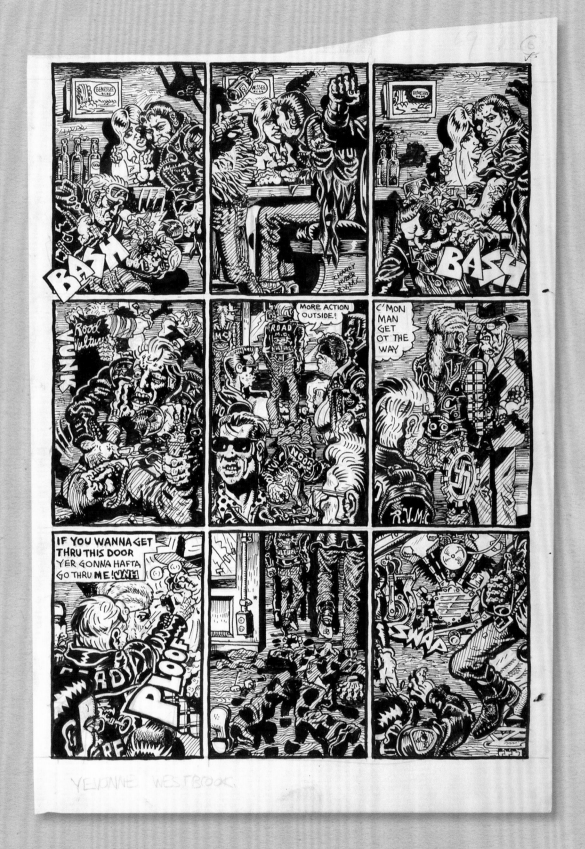

Brush, pen, and ink | 10 × 13 inches

Manuel "Spain" Rodriguez was a member of the prestigious *Zap* crew. This densely packed page, combining the street violence and artistry that Rodriguez is known for, was published in *Zap* no. 6. Rodriguez's evocation of and commitment to class warfare fueled much of his work, especially Trashman. His most recent accomplishment is *Che*, a 2008 graphic novel based on the life of Che Guevara.

Spain Rodriguez

Subvert no. 1, cover, 1970; Opposite: "The Origin of Trashman," 1970

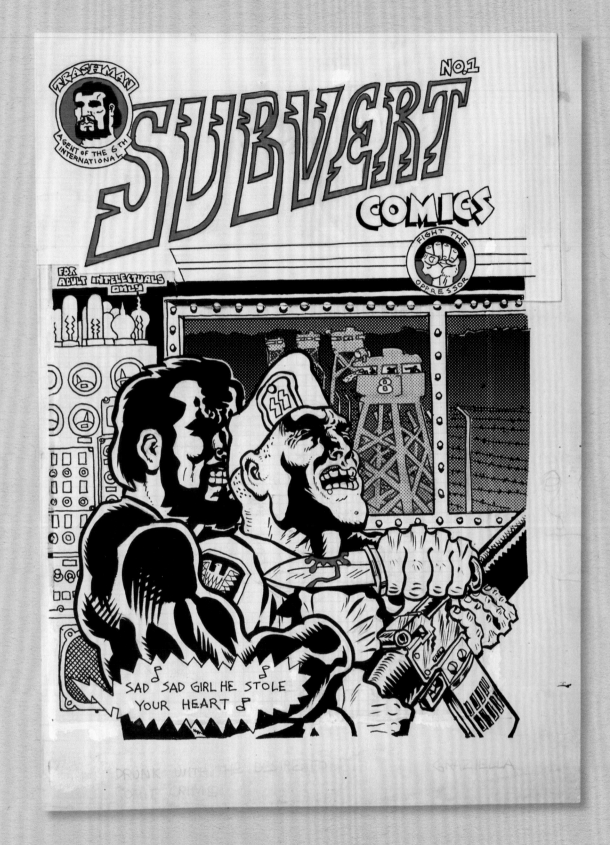

Brush, pen, and black and red ink with Zip-A-Tone | 8¼ × 11½ inches

Trashman, depicted as "hero of the revolution," partly reflects Rodriguez's wild early years as a biker in the Road Vultures (Buffalo, New York). Rodriguez was also among the most political of the underground cartoonists. He was a prime mover in establishing the United Cartoon Workers of America, an artists' union that he briefly tried to affiliate with the vestigial International Workers of the World in San Francisco.

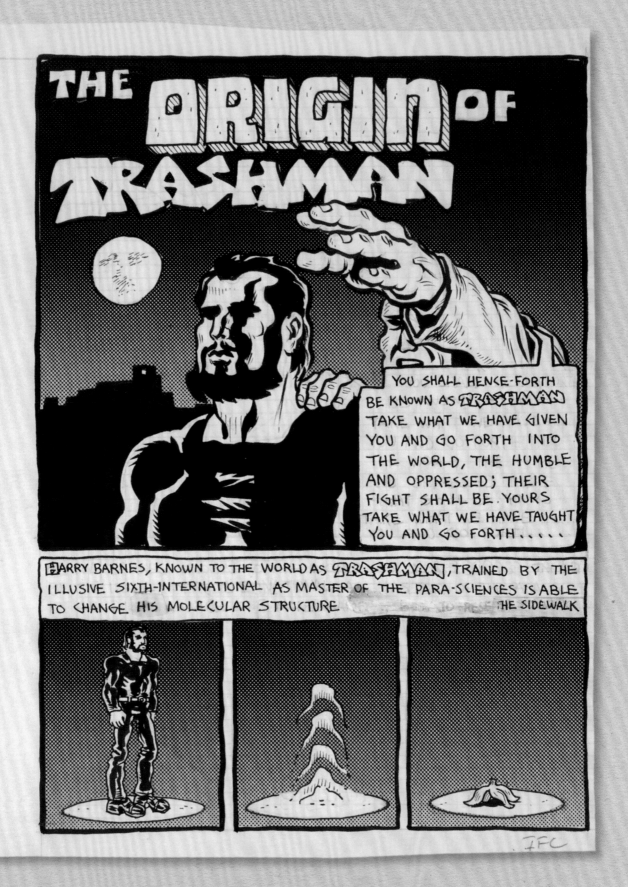

Brush, pen, and ink with Zip-A-Tone | 7½ × 10½ inches

Trashman ("Agent of the 6th International") was probably the most overtly revolutionary character in underground comix. There was nothing subtle about Trashman's efforts to violently overthrow the oppressive fascistic establishment, perceived by many readers in the seventies to be Nixonian in nature. This page from *Subvert* no. 1 is in the tradition of revealing the "origin" of comic book characters.

Sharon Rudahl
"Sex Welfare Benefits," 1975

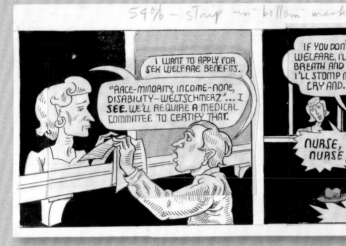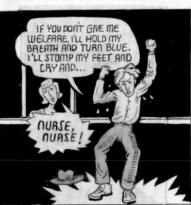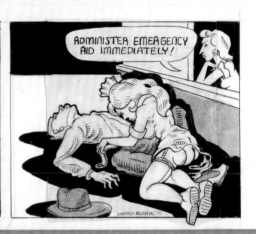

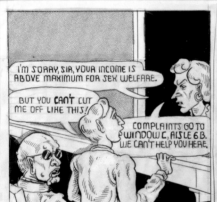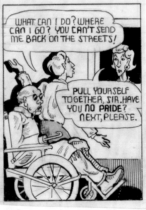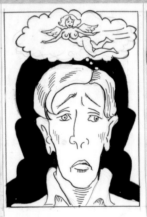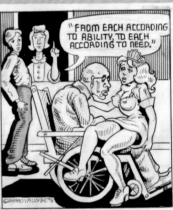

Pen and ink | each 14¼ × 4½ inches

Sharon Rudahl was one of the earliest women underground cartoonists, the solo creator of *Crystal Night*, and a contributor to *Wimmen's Comix* and numerous other titles. Among the more political artists, one of her strips discussed her oblique connection to the infamous math-research building bombing in Madison, Wisconsin. In 2007 the New Press published her graphic novel *A Dangerous Woman: The Graphic Biography of Emma Goldman*. In "Sex Welfare Benefits," done in a daily strip format for *Comix Book*, sex workers are part of America's future welfare system.

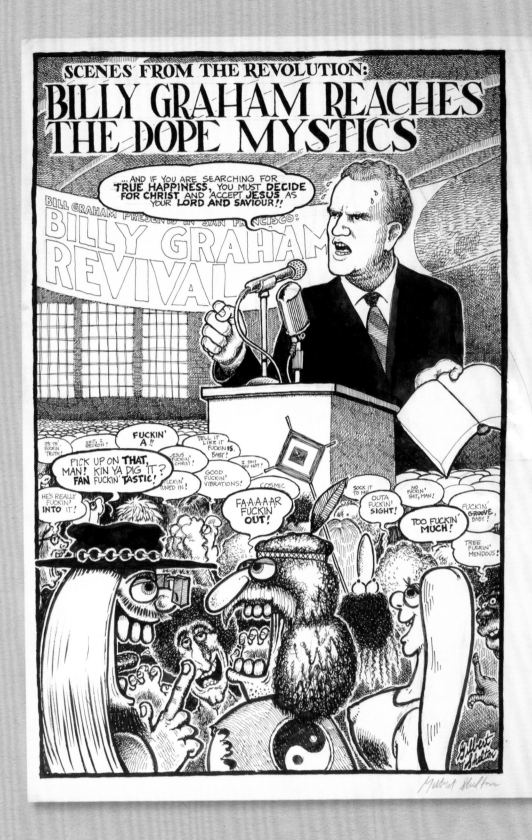

Pen and ink | 15 × 20 inches

In 1969 *Radical America Komiks*, a magazine published by SDS (Students for a Democratic Society) and edited by Paul Buhle, contacted Shelton to help organize an all-comics issue of the political journal. Shelton edited the book, drew the cover, and also printed it at Rip Off Press in San Francisco, where Shelton was a founding partner. In this scene of cultural disconnect, zoned-out hippies are part of the crowd at one of Rev. Graham's revivals. Graham, an advisor to several presidents along with his evangelical responsibilities, was seen as fair game on the political scene.

GILBERT SHELTON

"The Fabulous Furry Freak Brothers: Mystery Drugs," 1970

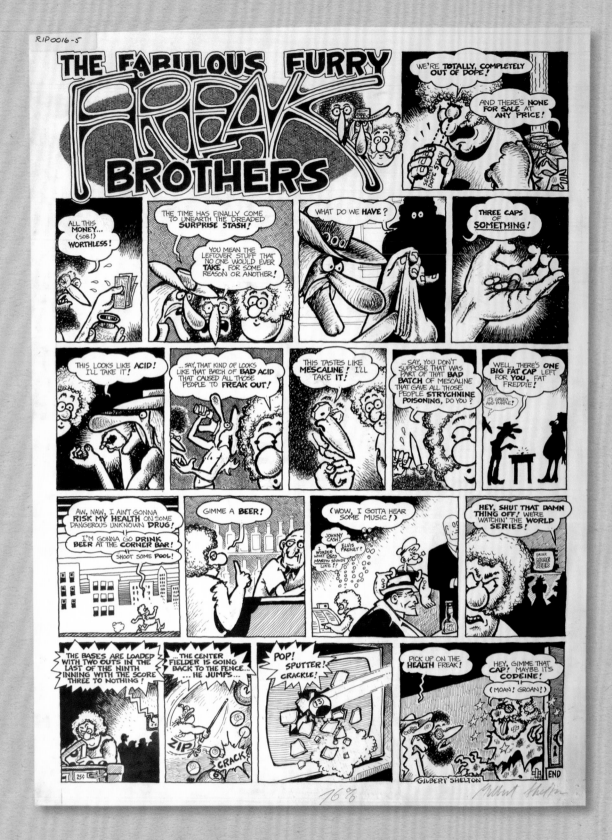

Pen and ink | 15 × 20 inches

The strong narrative sense of *The Fabulous Furry Freak Brothers*, coupled with more-than-clever drawings, helped to create a massive audience for Gilbert Shelton's best-known creation. The cumulative circulation of this series reached well into seven figures. Sometimes called "The Marx Brothers of comix," the dope-fueled adventures of the three hirsute brothers (Phineas, Fat Freddy, and Freewheeling Frank) eventually reached a global audience. In this page from the first issue of *Freak Brothers*, some of the elements that would continue through the decades were apparent.

Gilbert Shelton, Paul Mavrides

The Fabulous Furry Freak Brothers no. 9, cover, 1985

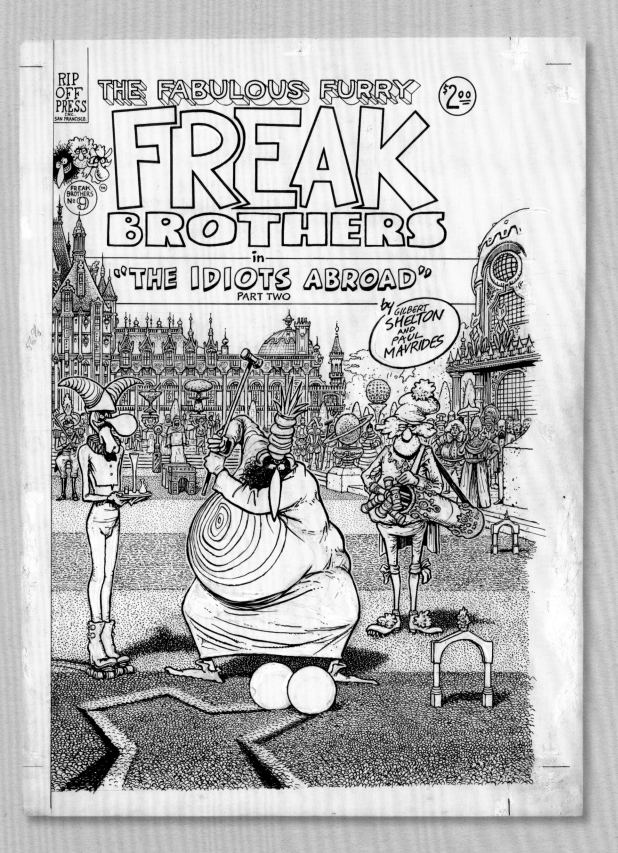

Pen and ink | 15 × 20 inches

By this point in his career, Gilbert Shelton was collaborating with Paul Mavrides to try to meet the demands of fans for his popular Rip Off Press series. Unlike monthly newsstand comic books, produced on an assembly-line basis, undergrounds were published erratically, only as quickly as the artist could—or chose to—produce the pages. This cover for their "Idiots Abroad" epic shows both the surreal nature of the humor and the artists' meticulous attention to detail (a telling explanation for the inability to publish with any frequency).

ART SPIEGELMAN

"Self-portrait with Characters," 1974; Opposite: *Snarf* no. 7, cover, 1976

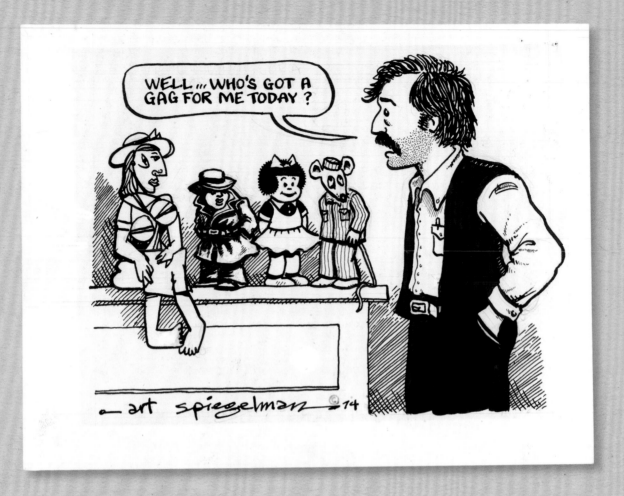

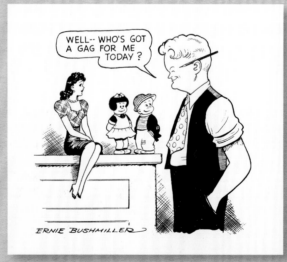

Pen and ink | 6¾ × 5¼ inches

Art Spiegelman is one of America's best-known artists, an unusual accomplishment for someone rooted in comics. Here Spiegelman draws himself with three of his own creations: an abstract Picasso-inspired woman (from *Ace Hole, Midget Detective*), Ace Hole himself, and a concentration camp mouse from *Maus*, along with Nancy, a character not created by him (and excoriated by many). The source for Spiegelman's parody, shown here, is a 1930s self-portrait by Ernie Bushmiller from *Comics and Their Creators*, with his syndicated characters Fritzi Ritz, Nancy, and Sluggo. Perhaps finding himself short on stationery, Spiegelman used the reverse side of his own drawing to write a letter to a colleague in 1974.

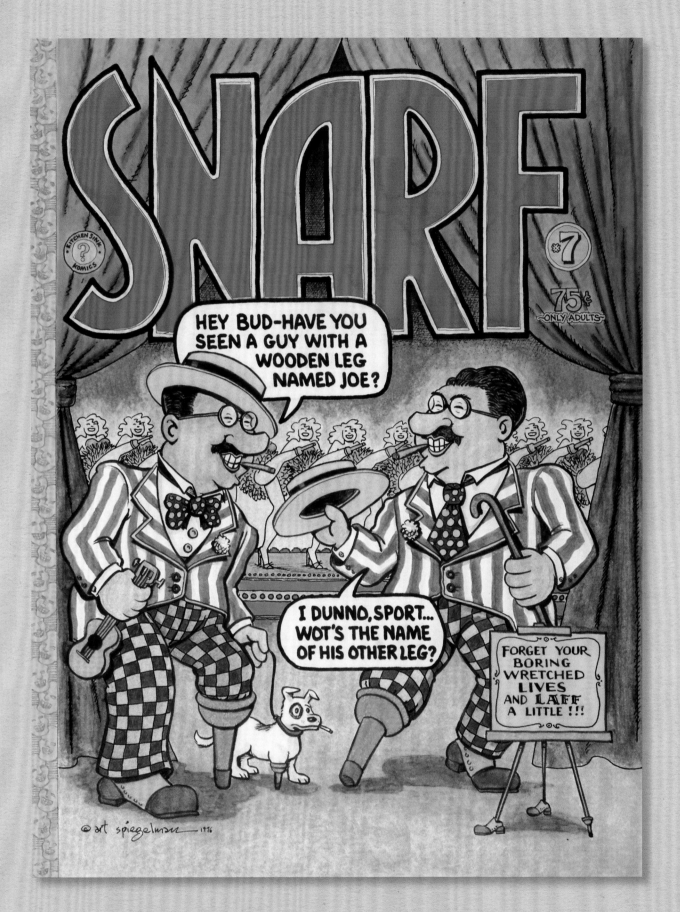

Pen and ink with mixed media | 15 × 19¾ inches

Born in Stockholm to Polish-Jewish refugees, Art Spiegelman grew up in New York, where he continues to work. Spiegelman's oeuvre crosses the boundaries of comics/comix to high art and back again. In the sixties, Spiegelman suffered a nervous breakdown from which he recovered and that he addressed in some of his underground comix. He is also known for clever visuals and wordplay, as in this Vaudeville-inspired peg-leg gag. His early work appeared in a number of titles, including *Bijou Funnies*, *Real Pulp*, *Young Lust*, *Bizarre Sex*, and *Sleazy Scandals of the Silver Screen*.

ART SPIEGELMAN
Maus preliminary drawings, 1971-72

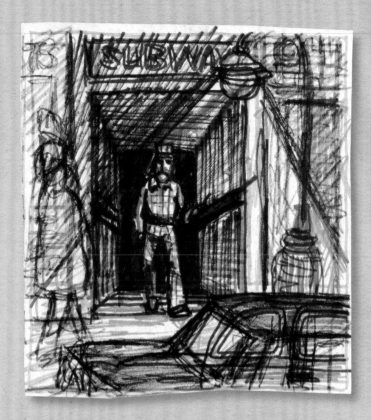

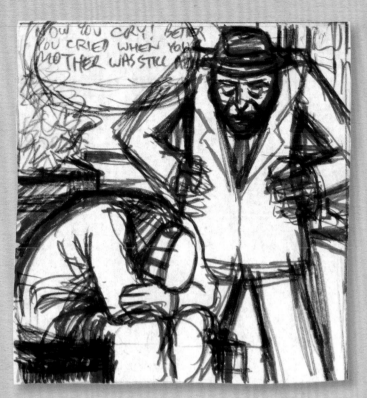

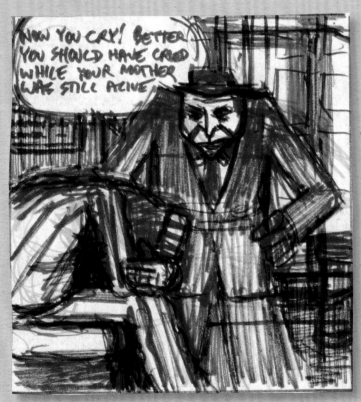

Overlapping color markers on tracing paper | Varying sizes

Subtitled "A Survivor's Tale," *Maus* began its cartoon existence as a brief story in the underground comic *Funny Aminals* in 1972. As Art Spiegelman expanded and serialized the story in *RAW* to book length, the power of the text and drawings grew dramatically. In addition to a Pulitzer Prize, *Maus* received numerous awards and accolades, acknowledging its value as a resource that allows everyone to understand both the horror of the Nazi regime and

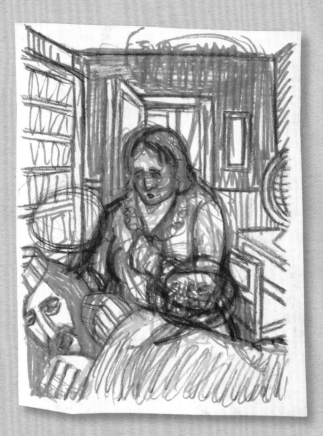
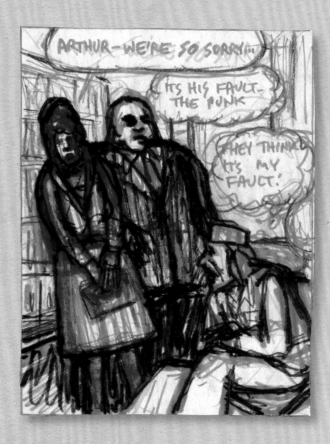
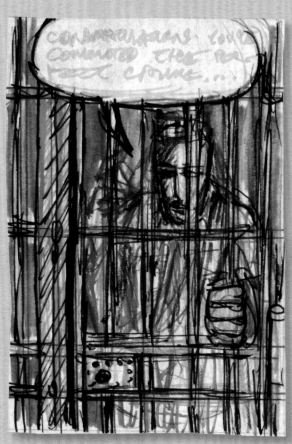
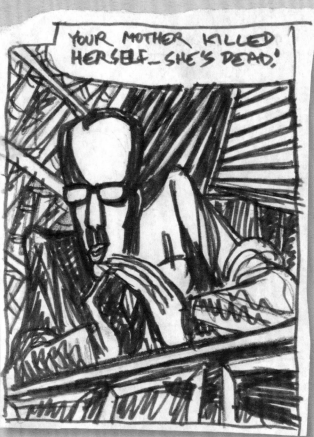

what it was like to live with parents who went through it. These preliminary drawings are from the "Prisoner on Hell Planet" section of the celebrated graphic novel. The buildup of panel composition from lighter to darker colors on tracing paper is a technique Spiegelman picked up from Harvey Kurtzman, an artist he greatly admired.

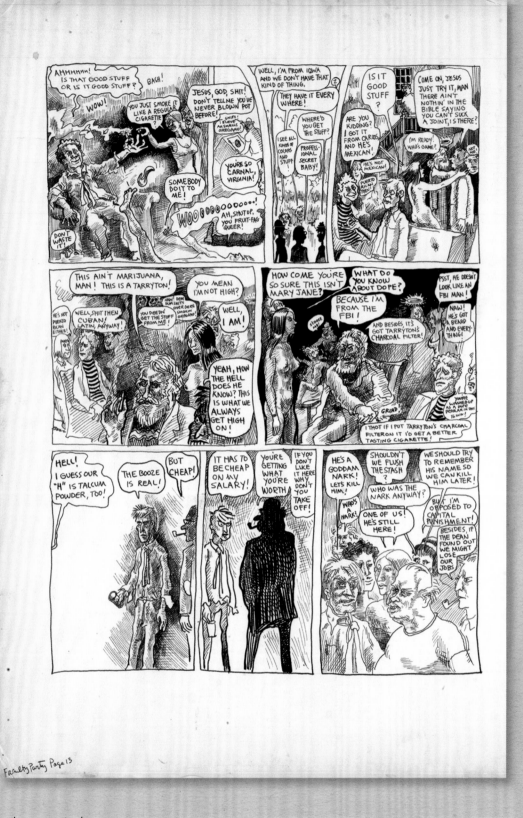

Pen and ink | each 10 × 15 inches

Religious themes, specifically Christian ones, have been a lifelong focus of Frank Stack's satire. In his earliest comix, *The Adventures of Jesus, The New Adventures of Jesus,* and *Jesus Meets the Armed Services,* published by Rip Off Press, the necessity of Stack's pseudonym, Foolbert Sturgeon, is obvious. One of the earliest of the underground cartoonists, he worked under this pen name in order to gain tenure and avoid persecution while living and teaching in the Bible Belt.

DAMNSHIT PISS FUCK! NO DOPE, NO BEER, NO HORS D'OEVRES! NO NOTHIN' NOW WHAT THE FUCK'RE WE GOING TO DO?
WHAT TIME IS IT?
2
WELL, IT WONT BE MUCH WITHOUT BEING STONED, BUT WE CAN PAIR OFF AND BALL!
WELL, LET'S SEE IF WE'VE GOT ENUF COUCHES!
WHAT HAPPENED TO THE COUCHES?
WE DON'T HAVE ANY COUCHES!
AND ALL THE REST OF THE FURNITURE?
CAWDS!
THE FLOOR'S ALL COVERED WITH BARF AND SHIT
YECH!
I GOT TO LAY DOWN IN THAT!
HEY! HERE'S A CLEAN PLACE!
WHAT ABOUT YOU, CHRIST? ARE YOU IN OR OUT?
LET'S EAT SOMETHING!
I'M TOO TIRED TO SCREW!
YOU'RE JUST A FAG!
THE STOVE'S STILL HERE!
TURN IT ON!
THE STOVE WON'T COME ON!
YOU HAVE TO LIGHT IT WITH A MATCH DUMBUTT!
BLOOOY!
DAWN!
I GUESS IT'S TIME TO LEAVE. I HAVE A CLASS IN 20 MINUTES
GOD! WHAT A BORE!
I THOUGHT HE'D NEVER LEAVE!
end
Foolbert Sturgeon
Faculty Party 14

"Wobblies!" 1979; Opposite: "My First Marijuana Experience!" 1984

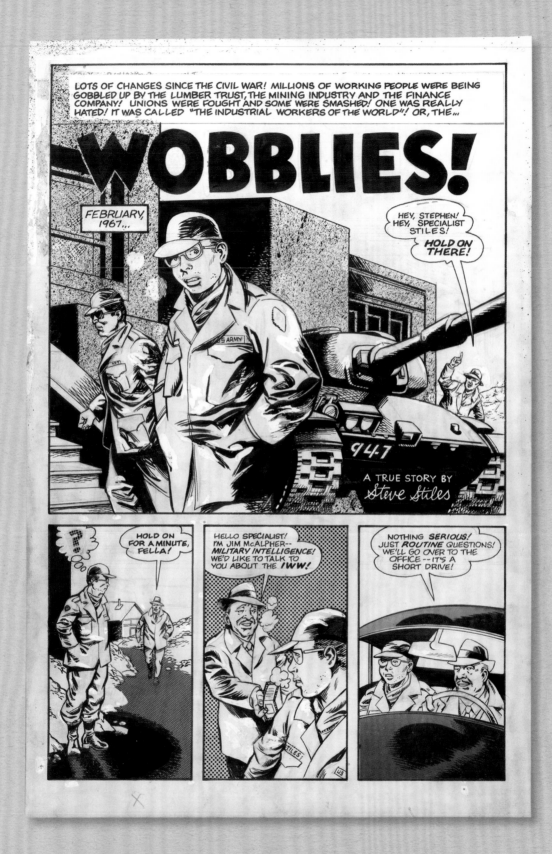

Pen and ink with Zip-A-Tone | 11 × 16½ inches

Steve Stiles graduated from New York's famed High School of Music and Art, where Harvey Kurtzman and other artists associated with *MAD* had gone before. Today he is best known as a science-fiction artist, but he was a prolific contributor to the undergrounds as well. In this splash page on the International Workers of the World (better known as the IWW), Stiles reminisces about his involvement with the "Wobblies." This story represents the use of history in the field and is also a surprisingly rare example of the overt Left politics discussed in underground comix.

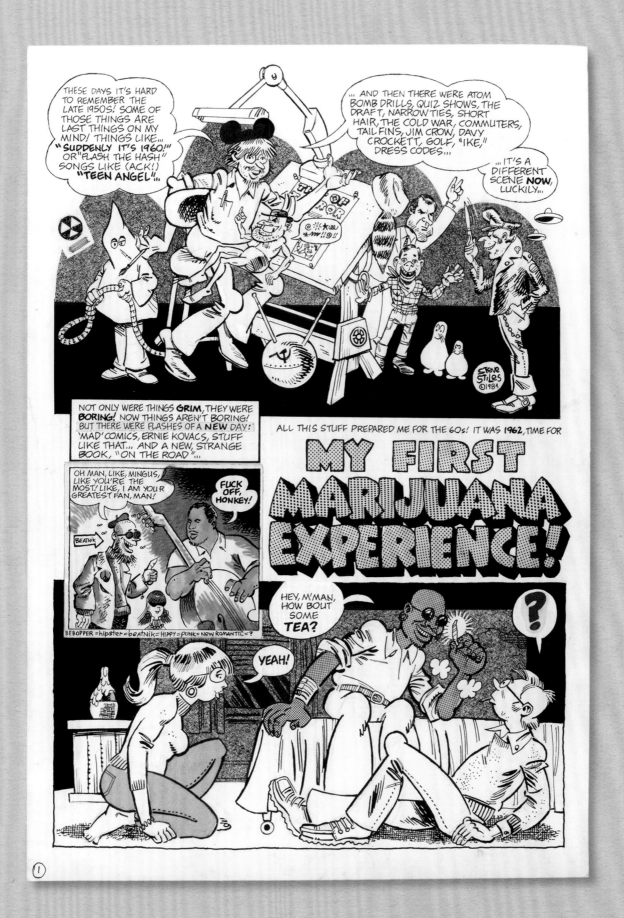

Pen and ink with Zip-A-Tone | 11½ × 17 inches

Stiles began his freelance career as a teenager, selling his first drawing to Paul Krassner's the *Realist*, and his work has appeared in children's books and many other places beyond the undergrounds. This page from an autobiographical story in *Dope Comix* details a common experience of the sixties and beyond. *Dope Comix* encouraged cartoonists to discuss and illustrate their personal experiences with mind-altering drugs, both pleasant and unpleasant—with Stiles decidedly in the former camp.

WILLIAM STOUT

Slow Death no. 8, cover, 1977

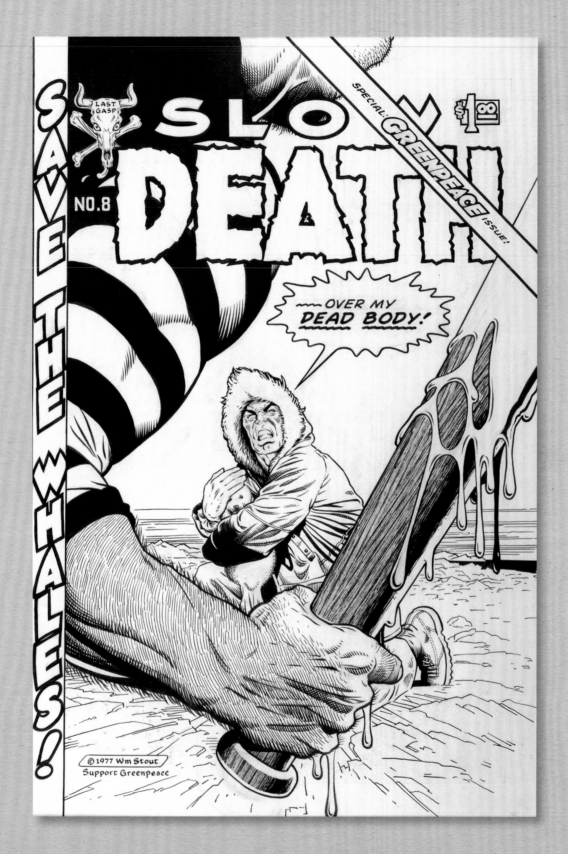

Brush and ink | 12 × 16 inches

Like Robert Williams and Rick Griffin, William Stout had formal art training at L.A.'s Chouinard Art Institute. After working with Harvey Kurtzman and Will Elder on "Little Annie Fanny," he entered the film business. His 1981 bestseller, *The Dinosaurs*, made Stout well known for prehistoric life reconstructions. Seventeen Stout murals are on permanent display in museums around the world. Here he dramatizes the killing of baby seals for their fur. Though undergrounds are often typecast for their sex and drug content, many contributors were early supporters of the environmental movement.

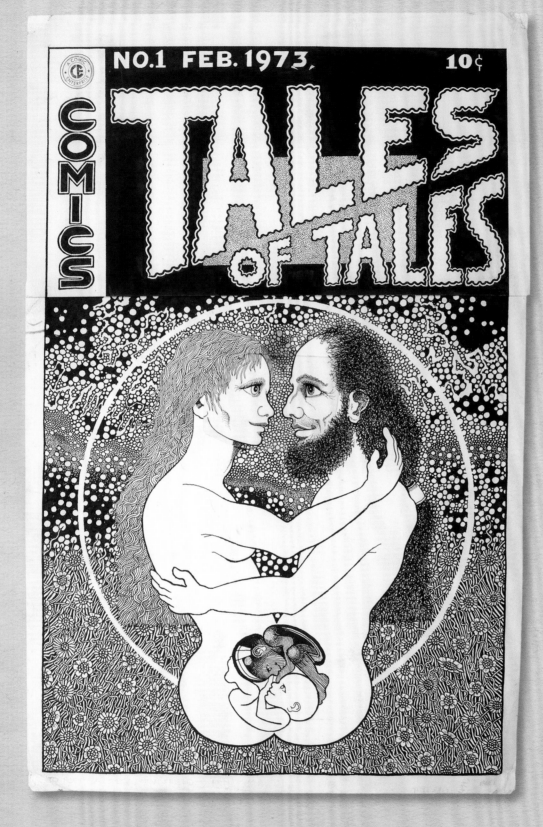

Pen and ink | 13 × 19 inches

John Thompson effectively cornered the non-linear/mystical niche of underground comix in solo titles such as *Tales From the Sphinx* and *The Kingdom of Heaven Is Within You*, primarily for the Print Mint. This unpublished cover of *Tales of Tales* no. 1 is a prime example of his intricate style, erotic/esoteric subject matter, and psychedelic imagery. Thompson was one of the few comix artists who also did political/editorial cartoons. His work in both areas was a staple of the leading underground newspapers of the day, including the *Los Angeles Free Press* and *Berkeley Barb*.

LARRY TODD

"Red Robot," 1972

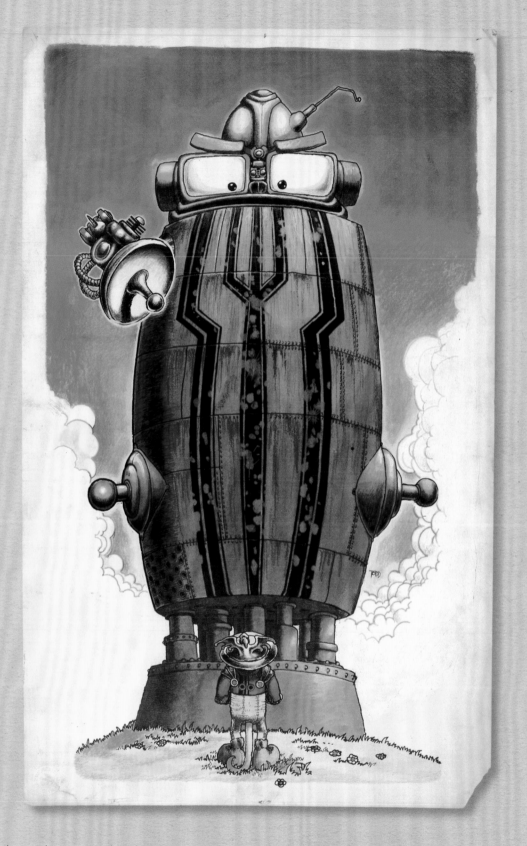

Brush, ink, and paint | 15 × 26 inches

Larry Todd was a friend of Vaughn Bode at Syracuse University, and later was an active member of the San Francisco group of underground cartoonists. He created the masthead for the short-lived the *Sunday Paper*, which offered readers something that looked like a traditional Sunday section, except it was filled with the work of Art Spiegelman, Gilbert Shelton, Willy Murphy, and others. Whether through his best-known *Dr. Atomic* comix series, early contributions to *Cherry Poptart*, or work on *Cobalt 60*, Todd brought his style and sensibility along with an ability to mimic.

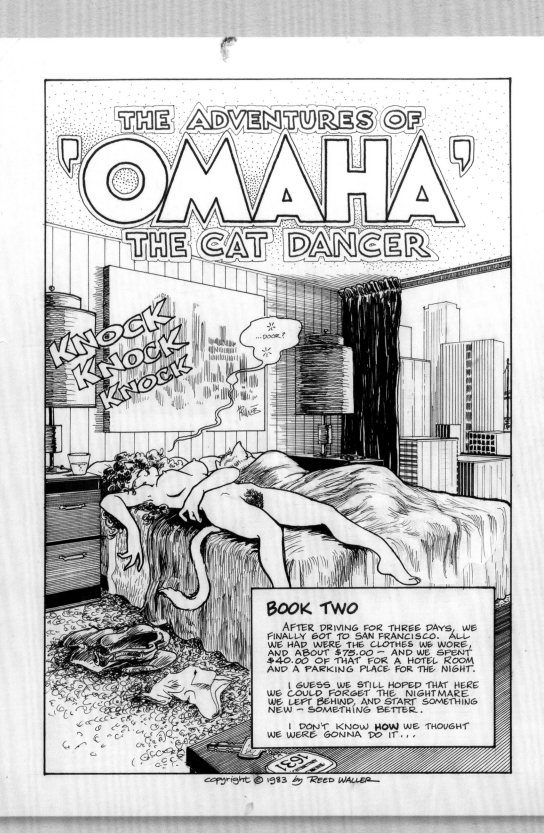

Pen and ink | 14 × 18 inches

Written as an ongoing erotic melodrama, the *Omaha* epic eventually came to fill eight collected volumes. *Omaha* was deeply informed by sex positive feminism. Drawn by Waller, a male, and written by Worley, a female, the anthropomorphic and sometimes sexually explicit strip was one of the more popular undergrounds, and the first to attract a sizable female audience. Also a magnet for obscenity charges, *Omaha* was busted in a historic 1986 case leading to the formation of the Comic Book Legal Defense Fund, a nonprofit organization defending First Amendment rights in the comics industry.

ROBERT WILLIAMS

"Dormasintoria," 1969

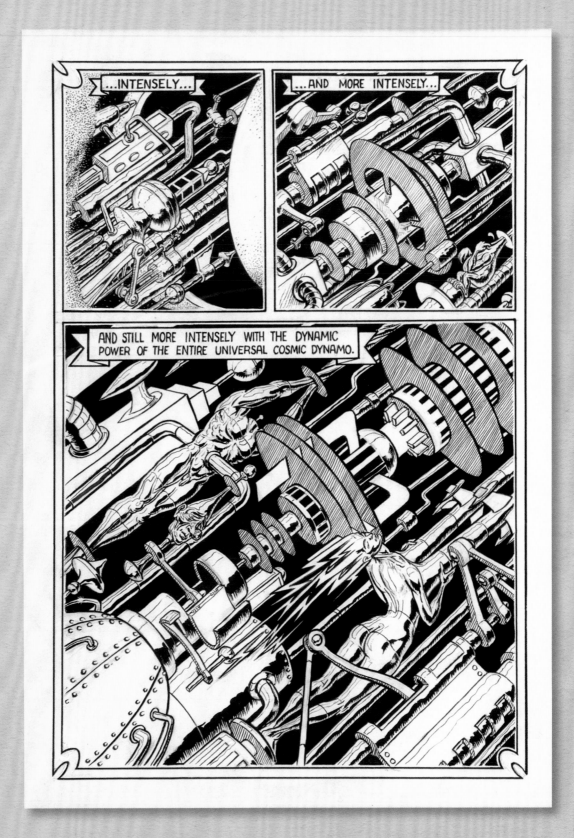

Brush, pen, and ink | each 9 × 12 inches

Sometimes described as the master of lowbrow art, Robert Williams was one of the earliest and most significant of the cartoonists who found their way to the freedom afforded by comix. Williams has described his attraction as rooted in love of especially graphic images married to a complete lack of constraints, as evident in "Dormasintoria," his first story for *Zap*, the premiere underground anthology. More recently Williams founded the influential *Juxtapoz Art & Culture Magazine*.

AND THEN!...
KABLOOWY
THAT, MY STAR-GAZING FRIEND, IS "THE BIG BANG THEORY!"
SHIVER ME VULVAS, MATEY!
...AND SO IT WAS, AS IT WAS TOLD BY THE OLD "MAN IN THE BOAT!"
END
ROBERT WILLIAMS

ROBERT WILLIAMS

Cocaine Comix no. 3, cover, 1981

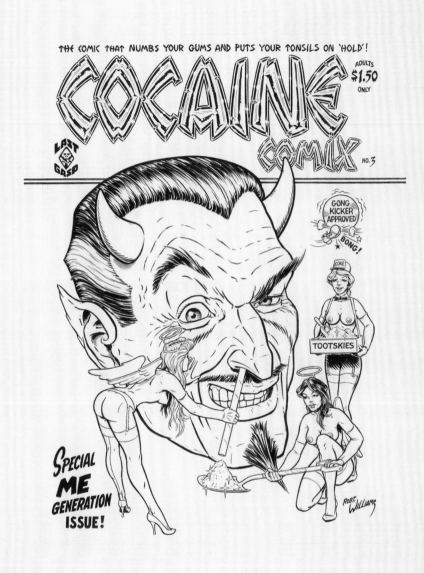

Brush and ink | 17 × 22 inches

Today Robert Williams is a highly regarded painter whose work routinely brings well into six figures, but his roots are in comix, where he was one of the key members of the closed shop comprising *Zap*. Williams began by drawing hot-rod cartoons for Ed "Big Daddy" Roth, then turned his attention to the larger world. His often-disturbing drawings have been collected in numerous books, one of whose titles indicates Williams's artistic trajectory, *Hysteria in Remission*. Satan is the featured character in this overtly drug-oriented series.

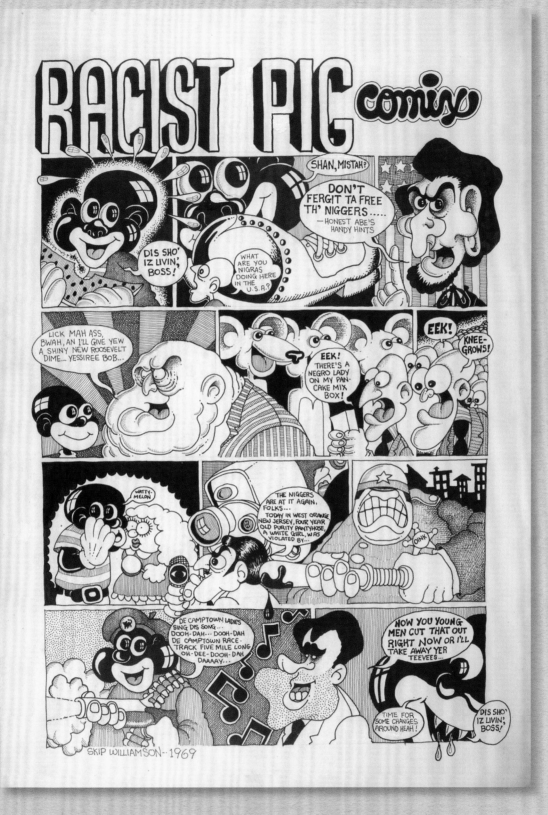

Pen and ink | 13 × 19½ inches

Mervyn "Skip" Williamson noted in an interview that his parents did not let him create comics, but they could not prevent him from reading them. As a teenager in the early sixties, Williamson had his first cartoon published in Harvey Kurtzman's *Help!* magazine and he never looked back. He moved to Chicago to collaborate on *Bijou Funnies*, one of the earliest of the undergrounds, with Jay Lynch. Politics were never far from Williamson's mind or pen as this piece from *Bijou* shows.

S. CLAY WILSON

"Head First," 1968; Opposite: "The Swap," 1974

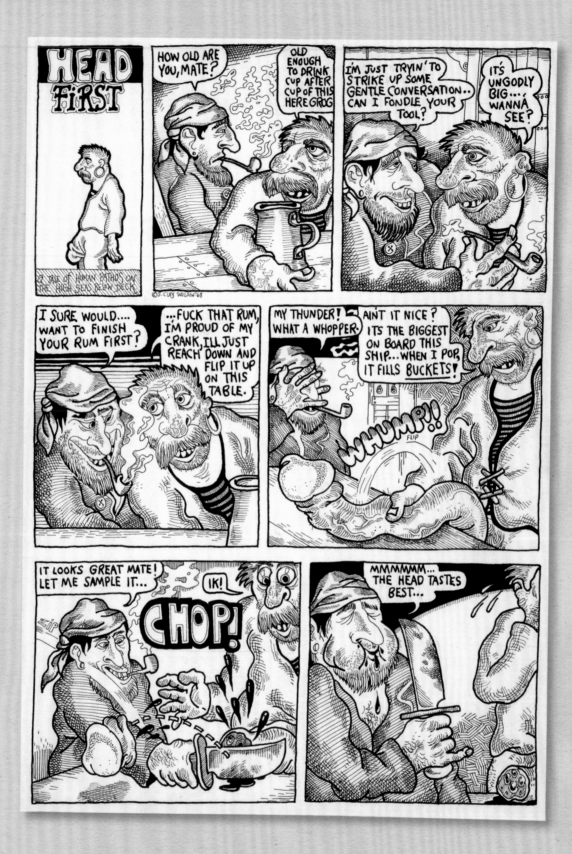

Pen and ink | 10¼ × 14½ inches

S. Clay Wilson, an unabashed exponent of sex and violence, was a seminal figure who helped make underground comix a cultural landmark. Born in Nebraska and trained as an army medic, Wilson headed west to San Francisco and met Charles Plymell, the original publisher of Robert Crumb's *Zap* no. 1. Wilson joined Crumb for the second issue and immediately liberated the medium with this audacious one-pager. As *Zap* colleague Victor Moscoso put it, "'Head First' blew the doors off the church."

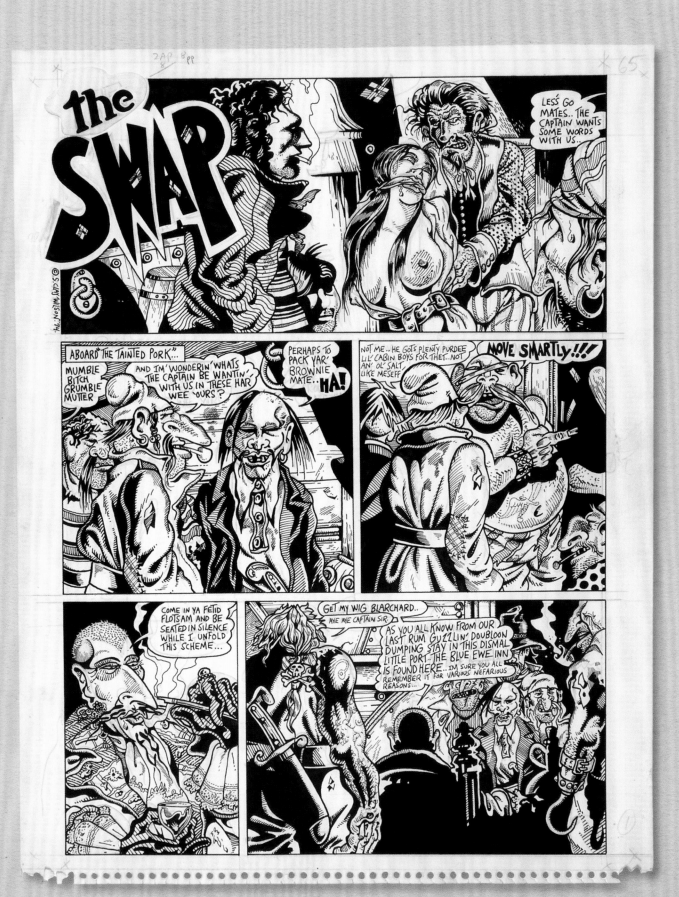

Brush, pen, and ink | 9½ × 11 inches

This splash page from *Zap* no. 8, in comparison to his first *Zap* contribution six years earlier, dramatizes Wilson's evolution from a simpler overall style to a denser page design, stronger balance of black and white, stylized lettering, and a more calligraphic line. What remains unchanged is the prevalence of sex and violence that is integral to Wilson's work. He astonished and sometimes frightened his fellow cartoonists, though they saw it as pushing, if not eviscerating, boundaries of taste. More than anyone, Wilson defined the boundaries of the medium.

LISTING OF ALL WORKS IN THE EXHIBITION

DIMENSIONS ARE IN INCHES; WIDTH PRECEDES HEIGHT

JOEL BECK (American, 1944–99)
"The Rise and Fall and Rise and Fall and Rise
and Fall of the American Revolution," 1972
Pen and ink, 10 × 16
Collection of Denis Kitchen

JOEL BECK (American, 1944–99)
"Various Cells of the Human Brain," 1974
Pen and ink, 14 ¼ × 20 ½
Collection of Denis Kitchen

JOEL BECK (American, 1944–99)
"One Dong's Family," from *Bizarre Sex* no. 5
(two pages), 1976
Pen and ink, 13 × 18 ½
Collection of Denis Kitchen

JOEL BECK (American, 1944–99)
Self-portrait for Famous Cartoonist
Button Series, 1974
Pen and ink on Bristol board, 2 ½ square
Collection of Denis Kitchen

VAUGHN BODE (American, 1941–75)
"Dis is a Bust!" from *Cheech Wizard* no. 5, 1972
Color markers, 9 ½ × 14 ¼
Collection of Eric Sack

VAUGHN BODE (American, 1941–75)
"Love is Thee," 1971
Color markers, 14 × 19
Collection of Eric Sack

VAUGHN BODE (American, 1941–75)
"Cheech Wizard: Da' Terminal Trick," 1975
Black and gray markers, 9 ½ × 14 ¼
Collection of Eric Sack

TIM BOXELL (American, b. 1950)
Commies From Mars: The Red Planet! no. 1,
cover, 1972
Brush and ink with Zip-A-Tone, 11 × 15
Collection of Denis Kitchen

ROGER BRAND (American, 1943–85);
JOEL BECK (American, 1944–99); and
KIM DEITCH (American, b. 1944)
Banzai! no. 1, cover, 1978
Brush, pen, and ink on Bristol board, 14 ½ × 23
Collection of Denis Kitchen

CHARLES BURNS (American, b. 1955)
Dope Comix no. 5, cover, 1982
Serigraph, signed, 24 × 27
Collection of Denis Kitchen

LESLIE CABARGA (American, b. 1954)
Comix Book no. 4, cover, 1976
Brush and ink with airbrushed color,
14 ¾ × 19
Collection of Eric Sack

LESLIE CABARGA (American, b. 1954)
Dope Comix no. 1, cover, 1978
Line art on acetate over airbrushed
background, 14 × 17 ¾
Collection of Denis Kitchen

DAN CLYNE (American, b. 1953) and
MERVYN "SKIP" WILLIAMSON
(American, b. 1944)
Hungry Chuck Biscuits Comics and Stories no. 1,
unpublished cover, 1971
Pen and ink with Zip-A-Tone on
illustration board, 12 × 15 ½
Collection of Denis Kitchen

RICHARD CORBEN (American, b. 1944)
"To Meet the Faces You Meet," 1972
Brush and ink with Zip-A-Tone
on illustration board, 12 × 15 ½
Collection of Denis Kitchen

RICHARD CORBEN (American, b. 1944)
Self-portrait for Famous Cartoonist
Button Series, 1974
Brush and ink on Bristol board, 6 square
Collection of Denis Kitchen

RICHARD CORBEN (American, b. 1944)
Reclining Nude, 1976
Cast resin, 11 × 12 × 4 ½
Collection of Denis Kitchen

ROBERT CRUMB (American, b. 1943)
Zap Comix no. 1, cover, silkscreen version,
1993/1967
Color serigraph, from an edition of
fourteen artist's proofs, 26 ¼ × 32 ¼
Collection of Denis Kitchen

ROBERT CRUMB (American, b. 1943)
"Meatball!" from *Zap* no. 0 (four pages), 1967
Pen and ink on Bristol board, each 7 ½ × 10 ¼
Collection of Eric Sack

ROBERT CRUMB (American, b. 1943)
Self-portrait, 1969
Pen and ink, 16 × 19
Collection of Denis Kitchen

ROBERT CRUMB (American, b. 1943)
Bijou Funnies no. 6, cover, 1971
Pen and ink, 7 ½ × 10 ¼
Collection of Eric Sack

ROBERT CRUMB (American, b. 1943)
Home Grown Funnies no. 2,
unpublished cover, 1972
Pen and ink on Bristol board, 11 × 14
Collection of Denis Kitchen

ROBERT CRUMB (American, b. 1943)
Snarf no. 6, cover, 1975
Pen and ink on board, 23 ¼ × 29 ¼
Collection of Denis Kitchen

ROBERT CRUMB (American, b. 1943)
"A Short History of America"
(15-panel version), 1993
Serigraph, artist's proof, signed, 19 × 22
Collection of Denis Kitchen

ROBERT CRUMB (American, b. 1943);
DON GLASSFORD (American, b. 1946);
JAY KINNEY (American, b. 1950);
DENIS KITCHEN (American, b. 1946);
JAY LYNCH (American, b. 1945);
JIM MITCHELL (American, b. 1949); and
MERVYN "SKIP" WILLIAMSON
(American, b. 1944)
"Let's Be Realistic Comics" jam, from
Mom's Homemade Comics no. 3 (two pages), 1971
Brush, pen, and ink with Zip-A-Tone on
illustration board, 13 × 19; 11 ½ × 17
Collection of Denis Kitchen

HOWARD CRUSE (American, b. 1944)
"Wendel: March on Washington"
(two pages), 1988
Pen and ink with Zip-A-Tone
on Bristol board, each 14 ½ × 20
Loaned by the artist

HOWARD CRUSE (American, b. 1944)
"Wendel: The Fagbasher" (two pages), 1989
Pen and ink with Zip-A-Tone
on Bristol board, each 14 ½ × 20
Loaned by the artist

KIM DEITCH (American, b. 1944)
"Be In" cover for the *East Village Other*,
October 11, 1968
Pen and ink on board, 12 × 14
Collection of Eric Sack

KIM DEITCH (American, b. 1944)
Self-portrait for Famous Cartoonist
Button Series, 1974
Pen and ink on Bristol board, 2 ¾ square
Collection of Denis Kitchen

WILL EISNER (American, 1917–2005)
Snarf no. 3, cover, 1972
Brush and ink on Bristol board, 9 × 13
Collection of Denis Kitchen

WILL ELDER (American, 1921–2008)
Snarf no. 10, cover, 1987
Ink, wash, and white watercolor on
illustration board, 12 ½ × 20
Collection of Denis Kitchen

WILL ELDER (American, 1921–2008)
Snarf no. 10, preliminary cover study, 1987
Pencil drawing, 6 ¾ × 10
Collection of Denis Kitchen

DREW FRIEDMAN (American, b. 1958)
"Jimmy Durante Boffs Starlets," 1984
Pen and ink, 8 × 11
Collection of Eric Sack

DON GLASSFORD (American, b. 1946);
DENIS KITCHEN (American, b. 1946);
WENDEL PUGH (American, b. 1943);
JAY LYNCH (American, b. 1945);
JIM MITCHELL (American, b. 1949);
BRUCE WALTHERS (American, b. 1944); and
MERVYN "SKIP" WILLIAMSON
(American, b. 1944)
"Group Self-portrait," 1971
Brush, pen, and ink with Zip-A-Tone on
illustration board, 11 ¾ × 9 ¼
Collection of Denis Kitchen

JUSTIN GREEN (American, b. 1945)
"Matriculation with Kiwi Brown and
the Statistics," from *Snarf* no. 6
(three pages), 1975
Pen, ink, rubber-stamp art, and
silkscreen on Bristol board, each 20 × 30
Collection of Denis Kitchen

JUSTIN GREEN (American, b. 1945)
"Zen Time," 1978
Pen and ink on Bristol board, 14 ¾ × 19
Collection of Denis Kitchen

RICHARD "GRASS" GREEN
(American, 1939–2002)
"Wild Man Meets Rubberoy," 1971
Pen and ink with Zip-A-Tone on
Bristol board, 11 ½ × 16
Collection of Denis Kitchen

RICK GRIFFIN (American, 1944–91)
"Fighting Eyeballs," 1968
Brush, pen, and ink, 11 × 16
Collection of Eric Sack

RICK GRIFFIN (American, 1944–91)
Zap no. 2, inside front cover, 1968
Brush, pen, and ink, 15 × 20
Collection of Eric Sack

BILL GRIFFITH (American, b. 1944)
Young Lust no. 3, cover, 1972
Pen and ink, 11 × 14
Collection of Eric Sack

BILL GRIFFITH (American, b. 1944)
Zippy Stories, cover, 1981
Brush, pen, and ink, 14 × 22
Collection of Eric Sack

GARY HALLGREN (American, b. 1945)
Air Pirates no. 2, cover, 1971
Brush, pen, and ink on Bristol board, 15 × 20
Loaned by the artist

RORY HAYES (American, 1949–83)
"The Midnight Monster," from *Insect Fear*
no. 3 (four pages), 1972
Pen and ink, each 9 × 12 ½
Collection of Eric Sack

RAND HOLMES (Canadian, 1942–2002)
A History Of Underground Comics,
wraparound cover, 1973
Brush and ink, 30 × 20
Collection of Eric Sack

RAND HOLMES (Canadian, 1942–2002)
"Great Job!" aka "Interrogation," 1977
Brush and ink on Craftint Duotone paper, 8 × 10

Loaned by the estate of the artist
GREG IRONS (American, 1947–84)
San Francisco Comic Book no. 3,
inside front cover, 1970
Pen and ink with Zip-A-Tone on
Bristol board, 11 × 14
Collection of Eric Sack

GREG IRONS (American, 1947–84)
Slow Death Funnies no. 1, cover, 1970
Brush, pen, and ink, 12 × 19
Collection of Eric Sack

JACK JACKSON (JAXON)
(American, 1941–2006)
Comanche Moon, 1976
Pen and ink with Zip-A-Tone, 11 ¼ × 17
Loaned by the estate of the artist

JACK JACKSON (JAXON)
(American, 1941–2006)
Portrait of Quanah Parker, 1985
Pen and ink with Zip-A-Tone, 14 ⅝ × 18 ¾
Loaned by the estate of the artist

JAY KINNEY (American, b. 1950)
"Say! What Ever Happened to the Counter-
Culture?," 1980
Pen and ink, tempera on blue line board
with acetate overlay, 10 × 15
Loaned by the artist

DENIS KITCHEN (American, b. 1946)
Bizarre Sex no. 1, cover, 1972
Pen and ink on illustration board, 14 × 16 ¾
Collection of Denis Kitchen

DENIS KITCHEN (American, b. 1946)
"The Birth of *Comix Book*," from
Comix Book no. 1, 1973
Brush, pen, and ink with Zip-A-Tone on
illustration board, 10 × 14
Collection of Denis Kitchen

DENIS KITCHEN (American, b. 1946)
"Major Arcana," from *Mondo Snarfo*, 1975
Brush and ink on illustration board,
12¼ square (3-D version also displayed,
with accompanying glasses)
Collection of Denis Kitchen

DENIS KITCHEN (American, b. 1946)
Bugle-American no. 216, fifth anniversary
cover, 1975
Pen and ink on illustration board, 11 ¼ × 13
Collection of Denis Kitchen

DENIS KITCHEN (American, b. 1946)
"Working in Geektown" from *Mondo
Snarfo*, 1978
Brush, ink, and Zip-A-Tone on illustration
board, 12 × 17
Collection of Denis Kitchen

DENIS KITCHEN (American, b. 1946)
"Rural Publishing," from *Twist* no. 2, 1988
Brush, ink, and Zip-A-Tone on
illustration board, 9 ¼ × 14
Collection of Denis Kitchen

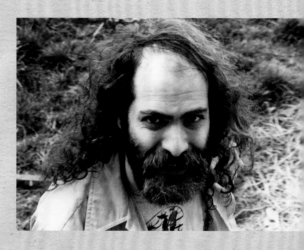

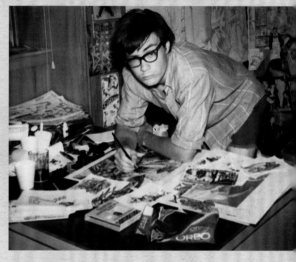

TOP | KIM DEITCH, 1972

BOTTOM | PETER POPLASKI
in his Princeton, Wisconsin, studio, 1973

ALINE KOMINSKY CRUMB
(American, b. 1948)
Self-portrait for Famous Cartoonist
Button Series, 1974
Pen and ink, 5 ¼ square
Collection of Denis Kitchen

ALINE KOMINSKY CRUMB
(American, b. 1948)
"Anatomy of The Bunch Body," 1981
Pen and ink on Bristol board, 12 × 13
Collection of Eric Sack

HARVEY KURTZMAN
(American, 1924–93)
Snarf no. 5, cover, 1972
Pen and ink on Bristol board, 11 ¼ × 14 ½
Collection of Denis Kitchen

BOBBY LONDON (American, b. 1950)
"Dirty Duck: Evils of Hashish," 1973
Pen and ink, 19 × 14
Collection of Eric Sack

JAY LYNCH (American, b. 1945)
Teen-Age Horizons Of Shangri-La no. 1,
cover, 1970
Pen and ink on Bristol board, 8 ¾ × 12
Collection of Denis Kitchen

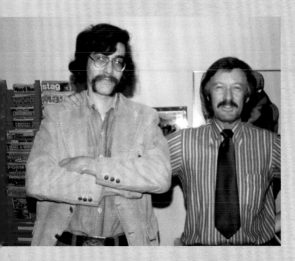

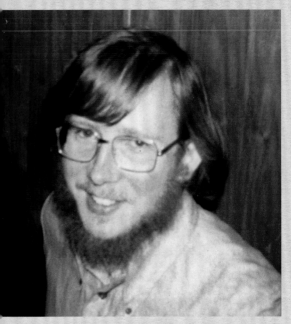

JAY LYNCH (American, b. 1945)
Chicago Seed, cover (unpublished by *Seed*), 1971
Pen and ink on Bristol board, 13 ¼ × 18 ¾
Collection of Denis Kitchen

JAY LYNCH (American, b. 1945)
Snarf no. 2, cover, 1972
Pen and ink on illustration board, 13 ½ × 18
Collection of Denis Kitchen

JAY LYNCH (American, b. 1945)
Dope Comix no. 3, cover, 1979
Pen and ink on illustration board, 14 × 18
Collection of Denis Kitchen

JIM MITCHELL (American, b. 1949)
"Reality Chick," 1971
Pen and ink with pencil shading
on illustration board, 18 ½ × 4 ¾
Collection of Denis Kitchen

JIM MITCHELL (American, b. 1949)
"Hello There!," 1971
Pen and ink with pencil shading on
illustration board, 18 ½ × 4 ¾
Collection of Denis Kitchen

JIM MITCHELL (American, b. 1949)
"Jim Mitchell's Pro Junior Comix"
(two pages), 1971
Pen and ink on Bristol board, each 13 ¼ × 17 ½
Collection of Denis Kitchen

VICTOR MOSCOSO
(American, born in Spain, b. 1936)
"Artists & Models" (four pages), 1978
Pen and ink, each 10 × 15
Collection of Eric Sack

WILLY MURPHY (American, 1937–76)
Cartoonists Co-Op Press promotional
cartoon, 1974
Pen and ink, 13 × 20 ½
Collection of Eric Sack

DAN O'NEILL (American, b. 1942)
"Buckey Bug," c. 1970
Pen, brush, and ink on Bristol board, 11 × 17
Collection of John Lind

DAN O'NEILL (American, b. 1942);
BOBBY LONDON (American, b. 1950);
GARY HALLGREN (American, b. 1945); and
SHARY FLENNIKEN (American, b. 1950)
Unpublished Air Pirates jam, 1975
Color markers, 20 × 15
Collection of Eric Sack

JIM OSBORNE (American, 1943–2001)
"Vultura," 1971
Pen and ink, 17 × 23
Collection of Eric Sack

HARVEY PEKAR (American, b. 1939) and
ROBERT CRUMB (American, b. 1943)
"Miracle Rabbis" (two pages, framed
together), 1982
Pen and ink on Bristol board, each 23 ¾ × 29 ¼
Collection of Denis Kitchen

PETER POPLASKI (American, b. 1951)
Comix Book no. 1, cover, 1973
Brush, pen, and ink with Zip-A-Tone
on illustration board, 13 ¼ × 16
Collection of Denis Kitchen

PETER POPLASKI (American, b. 1951)
Corporate Crime Comics no. 2, cover, 1979
Brush, pen, and ink with Zip-A-Tone
on illustration board, 15 ½ × 19 ½
Collection of Denis Kitchen

JOHN POUND (American, b. 1952)
Dope Comix no. 2, cover, 1978
Brush, ink, and gouache on illustration
board, 16 × 22
Collection of Eric Sack

SYLVIE RANCOURT (Canadian, b. 1959)
Self-portrait, 1990
Enamel paint on wood, 8 × 12 × ⅝
Collection of Denis Kitchen

TED RICHARDS (American, b. 1946)
"Travel on the Astral Plane," 1976
Pen and ink, 12 ¼ × 18 ½
Collection of Eric Sack

TRINA ROBBINS (American, b. 1938)
"One Flower Child's Search for Love"
(five pages), 1973
Brush, pen, and ink with Zip-A-Tone
on Bristol board, each 10 × 15
Collection of Denis Kitchen

TRINA ROBBINS (American, b. 1938)
Self-portrait for Famous Cartoonist
Button Series, 1974
Brush and ink on Bristol board, 5 ½ square
Collection of Denis Kitchen

MANUEL "SPAIN" RODRIGUEZ
(American, born in Mexico, b. 1940)
"The Origin of Trashman," 1970
Brush, pen, and ink with Zip-A-Tone, 7 ½ × 10 ½
Collection of Eric Sack

MANUEL "SPAIN" RODRIGUEZ
(American, born in Mexico, b. 1940)
Subvert no. 1, cover, 1970
Brush, pen, and black and red ink
with Zip-A-Tone, 8 ¼ × 11 ½
Collection of Eric Sack

MANUEL "SPAIN" RODRIGUEZ
(American, born in Mexico, b. 1940)
"Evening at the Country Club," from *Zap*
no. 6, 1971
Brush, pen, and ink on Bristol board, 10 × 13
Collection of Eric Sack

SHARON RUDAHL (American, b. 1947)
"Sex Welfare Benefits" (two pages), 1975
Pen and ink on Bristol board, each 14 ½ × 4 ½
Collection of Denis Kitchen

GILBERT SHELTON (American, b. 1940)
"Wonder Wart-Hog," from Harvey Kurtzman's
Help!, 1963
Pen and ink with Zip-A-Tone on
illustration board, 10 × 14 ¼
Loaned by the estate of Harvey Kurtzman

GILBERT SHELTON (American, b. 1940)
"Scenes from the Revolution: Billy Graham
Reaches the Dope Mystics," 1969
Pen and ink, 15 × 20
Collection of Eric Sack

GILBERT SHELTON (American, b. 1940)
"The Fabulous Furry Freak Brothers: Mystery
Drugs," 1970
Pen and ink, 15 × 20
Collection of Eric Sack

GILBERT SHELTON (American, b. 1940)
Self-portrait for Famous Cartoonist
Button Series, 1974
Pen and ink on letterhead, 6 × 8
Collection of Denis Kitchen

GILBERT SHELTON (American, b. 1940) and
PAUL MAVRIDES (American, b. 1952)
Fabulous Furry Freak Brothers no. 9, cover, 1985
Pen and ink, 15 × 20
Collection of John Lind

GILBERT SHELTON (American, b. 1940) and
DAVE SHERIDAN (American, 1944–82)
"Fat Freddy's Cat and his Friends," from
Fabulous Furry Freak Brothers, 1974
Pen and ink on illustration board, 13 ½ × 20 ¼
Collection of Denis Kitchen

GILBERT SHELTON (American, b. 1940) and
DAVE SHERIDAN (American, 1944–82)
Fabulous Furry Freak Brothers no. 4, cover, 1975
Painting, 15 × 20
Collection of Eric Sack

ART SPIEGELMAN
(American, born in Sweden, b. 1948)
Snarf no. 7, cover, 1976
Pen and ink with mixed media, 15 × 19 ¾
Collection of Eric Sack

ART SPIEGELMAN
(American, born in Sweden, b. 1948)
"Self-portrait with Characters" (framed
with parody source listed below), 1974
Pen and ink on illustration board, 6 ¾ × 5 ¼
Collection of Denis Kitchen

ERNEST PAUL "ERNIE" BUSHMILLER, JR.
(American, 1905–82)
"Self-portrait with Characters,"
from *Comics and Their Creators*, 1942
Book tearsheet, 4 square
Collection of Denis Kitchen

ART SPIEGELMAN
(American, born in Sweden, b. 1948)
"Pluto's Retreat," from *Bizarre Sex* no. 8, 1980
Hand-colored and retouched Photostat, 9 × 12
Collection of Denis Kitchen

ART SPIEGELMAN
(American, born in Sweden, b. 1948)
"Three Mice," 1993
Lithograph, no. 6 in edition of 8,
signed, 4 ¼ × 6 ½
Collection of Denis Kitchen

ART SPIEGELMAN
(American, born in Sweden, b. 1948)
Maus preliminary drawings, 1971–72
Overlapping color markers on tracing
paper, varying sizes
Collection of Denis Kitchen

FRANK STACK (Foolbert Sturgeon)
(American, b. 1937)
"Jesus Goes to a Faculty Party" (four pages
on two boards), 1972
Pen and ink on illustration board, each 10 × 15
Loaned by the artist

DAN STEFFAN (American, b. 1953)
"Marijuana, a.k.a. Leaf, Boo, Muggles et al,"
from *Dope Comix* no. 5, 1984
Brush and ink on illustration board, 9 × 12
Collection of Denis Kitchen

STEVE STILES (American, b. 1943)
"Wobblies!," 1979
Brush and ink with Zip-A-Tone
on illustration board, 11 × 16 ½
Collection of Denis Kitchen

STEVE STILES (American, b. 1943)
"My First Marijuana Experience!"
(two pages), 1984
Brush, pen, and ink with Zip-A-Tone on
illustration board, each 11 ½ × 17
Collection of Denis Kitchen

WILLIAM STOUT (American, b. 1949)
Slow Death no. 8, cover, 1977
Brush and ink on illustration board, 12 × 16
Collection of Eric Sack

JOHN THOMPSON (American, b. 1945)
Tales of Tales no. 1, unpublished cover, 1973
Pen and ink, 13 × 19
Collection of Eric Sack

LARRY TODD (American, b. 1948)
"Red Robot," 1972
Brush, ink, and paint, 15 × 26
Collection of Eric Sack

REED WALLER (American, b. 1949) and
KATE WORLEY (American, 1958–2004)
"The Adventures of Omaha The Cat
Dancer," 1983
Pen and ink on Bristol board, 14 × 18
Collection of Denis Kitchen

ROBERT WILLIAMS (American, b. 1943)
"Dormasintoria" (four pages), 1969
Brush, pen, and ink, each 9 × 12
Collection of Eric Sack

ROBERT WILLIAMS (American, b. 1943)
Cocaine Comics no. 3, cover, 1981
Brush and ink, 17 × 22
Collection of Eric Sack

MERVYN "SKIP" WILLIAMSON
(American, b. 1944)
"Racist Pig Comix," 1969
Pen and ink on illustration board, 13 × 19 ½
Collection of Eric Sack

MERVYN "SKIP" WILLIAMSON
(American, b. 1944)
"Capitol Hill Comix," 1971
Pen and ink on illustration board, 11 ½ × 18 ½
Collection of Denis Kitchen

S. CLAY WILSON (American, b. 1941)
"Head First," from *Zap* no. 2, 1968
Pen and ink, 10 ¼ × 14 ½
Collection of Eric Sack

S. CLAY WILSON (American, b. 1941)
"The Swap" (splash page), from *Zap* no. 8, 1974
Brush, pen, and ink, 9 ½ × 11
Collection of Eric Sack

S. CLAY WILSON (American, b. 1941) and
MERVYN "SKIP" WILLIAMSON
(American, b. 1944)
"The Checkered Demon Meets
Snappy Sammy Smoot," 1988
Color serigraph with dual signatures;
no. 226 of 250, 30 × 22
Collection of Denis Kitchen

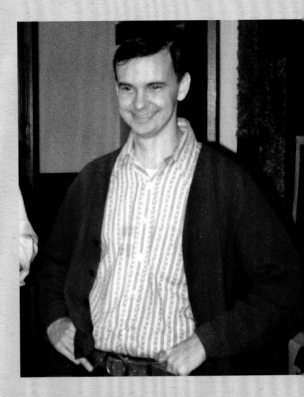

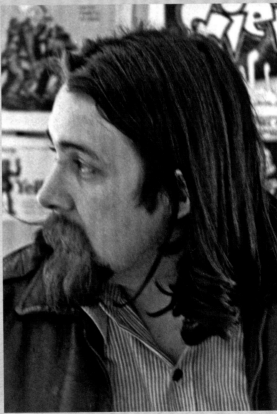

TOP | RICHARD CORBEN
in his Missouri home, 1976

BOTTOM | S. CLAY WILSON, 1973

INDEX

Page numbers in italics refer to illustrations.

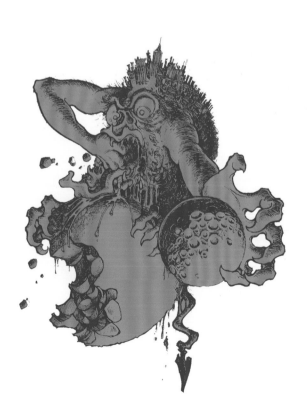

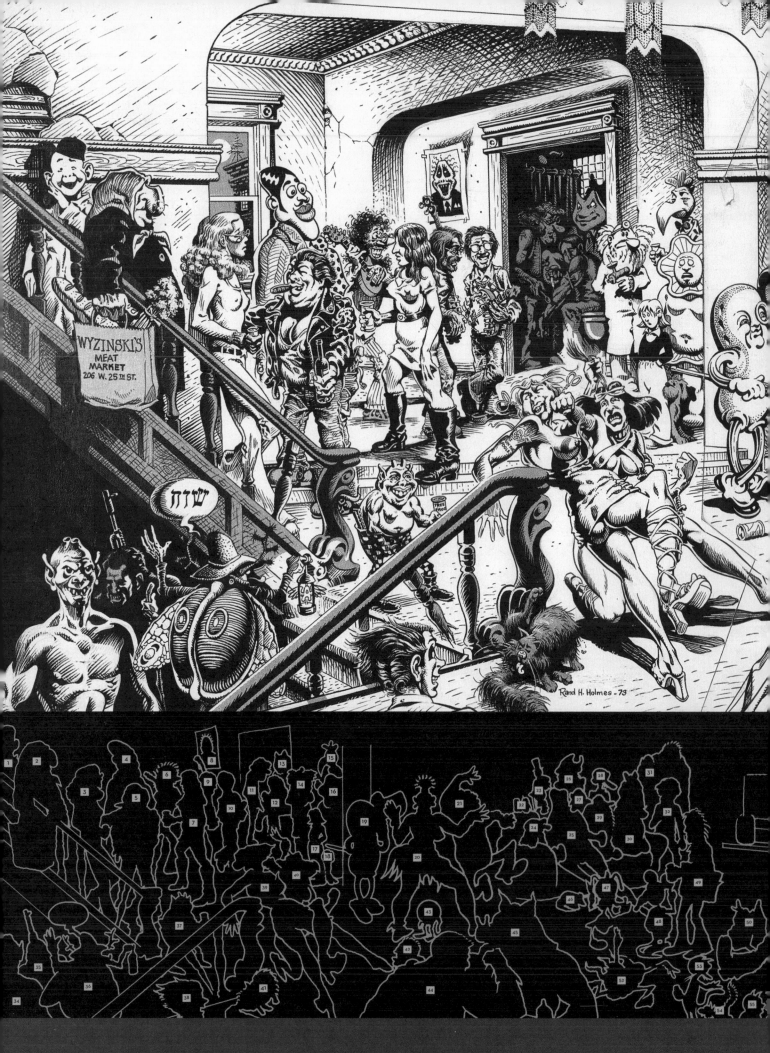

RAND HOLMES depicted a variety of cartoon characters and cartoonists partying in his wraparound cover for Mark Estren's *A History of Underground Comix* (Straight Arrow Books, 1973). Here's a breakdown of who's who…